SHORT CUTS

INTRODUCTIONS TO FILM STUDIES

T0324288

SHORT CUTS

INTRODUCTIONS TO FILM STUDIES

FOR A COMPLETE LIST OF TITLES IN THE SERIES, PLEASE SEE PAGES 151–152.

THE POP MUSICAL

SWEAT, TEARS, AND TARNISHED UTOPIAS

ALBERTO MIRA

WALLFLOWER

NEW YORK

Wallflower Press is an imprint of Columbia University Press
Columbia University Press
Publishers Since 1893
New York   Chichester, West Sussex
cup.columbia.edu

Library of Congress Cataloging-in-Publication Data

Names: Mira, Alberto, author.
Title: The pop musical : sweat, tears, and tarnished utopias / Alberto Mira.
Description: New York : Wallflower, [2021] | Series: Short cuts |
    Includes bibliographical references and index.
Identifiers: LCCN 2021011992 (print) | LCCN 2021011993 (ebook) | ISBN 9780231191234
    (trade paperback) | ISBN 9780231549295 (ebook)
Subjects: LCSH: Musical films—United States—History and criticism. | Popular music—
    Social aspects—United States—History. | Motion pictures and music.
Classification: LCC PN1995.9.M86 M537 2021 (print) | LCC PN1995.9.M86 (ebook) |
    DDC 791.43/6—dc23
LC record available at https://lccn.loc.gov/2021011992
LC ebook record available at https://lccn.loc.gov/2021011993

Columbia University Press books are printed on permanent and durable acid-free paper.
Printed in the United States of America

Cover image: *Rocketman* (2019). Paramount Pictures/Photofest

CONTENTS

ACKNOWLEDGMENTS

I am grateful to Yoram Allon, for embracing the possibilities of the project, and to Ryan Groendyk, my editor at Columbia University Press, for his support and his patience. Thanks to Kathryn Jorge for sterling support through the final stages of this book and also to Maddy Hamey-Thomas for insightful attention and suggestions to the manuscript during the copyediting process. I am also indebted to the anonymous reviewers for several stages of this book: they helped me clarify ideas and, even more importantly, think about future work in terms of the directions that could be taken next. The expert comments of my friends and colleagues Empar Barranco, Cora Pearlman, and Rosi Song helped to further shape the final version. The last stages of this volume hit the wall of the Covid lockdowns and closures, and checking materials became slow and difficult. I am grateful to Jaap Kooijman, who helped me with essential material.

I am lucky to work with a wonderful group of colleagues at Oxford Brookes University, who are an inspiration and an example. Special thanks to Daniela Treveri-Gennari, Gov Chandran, Lindsay Steenberg, Paolo Russo, James Cateridge, and Warren Buckland.

Musicals have been my passion since childhood and writing *The Pop Musical* has been part of a journey to understand the genre's continuing hold on me, as well as to broaden my horizons in terms of the kinds of music the genre can engage with. This love has been nurtured through the years by friends, internet groups, and mentors, and has been shaped by the work of such insightful academic fans of the genre such as Richard Dyer, to whose work I owe more than he can possibly realize. Most of the writing took place at my London house on Great Russell Street. Through the years, the place has been a haven for artists and writers. For me, everybody there is family, and their encouragement has been crucial to keep me going.

Finally, a project so deeply rooted in my life is indebted to my partner Joan Matabosch, who has put up with odd choices for home viewing and unexpected outbursts of Motown classics.

INTRODUCTION

The Hollywood Musical Is Dead.
Long Live the Hollywood Musical!

> If we view the Hollywood musical as one phase in the history of musical entertainment, we must refute the commonly held belief that the musical declined or died out in the 1950s. Instead we must see that the musical was transformed as the industry was transformed, with the positive reflexive function being transferred to the new mass medium, television.
> —Jane Feuer, *The Hollywood Musical*

It has become an academic cliché: by the 1980s the classical Hollywood musical was considered defunct. So it was time for an inventory of its legacy. Several coffee-table books, like Ted Sennet's lavish *Hollywood Musicals* or Clive Hirschhorn's comprehensive *The Hollywood Musical* (both published in 1981) or John Kobal's *Gotta Sing, Gotta Dance!* (a revised edition came out in 1983) itemized its glories. Academia also, including distinguished figures such as Richard Dyer (1977), Thomas Schatz (1981), Jane Feuer (1982), Peter Evans and Bruce Babington (1985), and Rick Altman (1987), paid serious attention to what had so far been considered second-rate, pure fan fodder, with little to offer to the cause of cinematic art. Intellectual inquiry started with fans becoming scholars. In a series of influential volumes and articles, these academic devotees discussed the musical's centrality in the classical Hollywood genre system as well as its specific, distinctive textures and meanings. Frameworks that have structured later discussions of the genre for decades were introduced in their essays: the musical's industrial underpinnings, its specific dual-focus structure, its utopian qualities, and its connections to folk art. The primary object of their inquiry was the genre in its "golden age phase" (roughly until the demise of the Freed Unit at MGM with the final flowering of *Gigi* in 1958), and interest seemed to wane when they considered the 1970s.

Still, films which made substantial narrative and dramatic use of song and dance kept large audiences entranced with entertainment like *The Rocky Horror Picture Show* (1975), *Grease* (1978), and *Cry Baby* (1990); whilst *Hair* (1979), *Fame* (1980), and *Velvet Goldmine* (1998) exhibited equal levels of originality and artistry, through their merging of music and narration, to earlier musicals.[1] New musical forms also pushed the musical into becoming socially aware, particularly in a short cycle of urban musicals that included *Wild Style* (1982) and *Beat Street* (1984), which featured the rising trend of street dance and reinterpreted the genre's folk discourse on community. This cycle was the first instance in a longer line that engaged with hip-hop culture and lasted for two decades and included *8 Mile* (2002), *Straight Outta Compton* (2015), and *All Eyez On Me* (2017). In 1987, after the first wave of hip-hop musicals ended, *Dirty Dancing* (1987) became one of the biggest hits of the decade, one in a long line of dance musicals that included the earlier *Flashdance* (1983) and the later *Step Up* series (2006, 2008, 2010, 2012, 2014, 2016, 2018). Broadway adaptations in these more recent decades, including *Little Shop of Horrors* (1986) and *Evita* (1996), gestured toward pop styles. And, one should add, some of the post-1987 Disney features included strong song scores from Broadway composers such as Stephen Schwartz and Alan Menken (*Pocahontas* [1995], *The Little Mermaid* [1989], *Hercules* [1997]) as well as pop musician performers like Elton John (*The Lion King* [1994]) and Phil Collins (*Tarzan* [1999]). Beginning in the late 1980s, a series of musical biopics explored the icons of the pop era: *Great Balls of Fire!* (1989), *The Doors* (1991), and *What's Love Got to Do with It* (1993), are examples of a trend that peaked in the following decades. The new century's first highlight was *Moulin Rouge!* (2001), a huge hit, combining old and new pop style compositions, which was followed by a new cycle of sleek Broadway adaptations, including *Dreamgirls* (2006) and *Hairspray*

(2008). Meantime, since the 1980s, as Feuer suggests in my opening quote, TV had been inspired by the Hollywood musical and had introduced a new media genre: the music video. MTV became a source of new links between pop songs and images. Musical features also became frequent on TV, as the success of *High School Musical* (2006) attests. And that was not all. When the new wave of serial fiction TV came about in the 2010s, some series incorporated the tropes and modes of the musical: *Glee* (2009–2015), *Smash!* (2012–2013), *Vinyl* (2016), *Nashville* (2012–2018), *Zooey's Extraordinary Playlist* (2020), and the hip-hop-themed *Empire* (2015–) and *The Get Down* (2016) are all examples of these.

Despite the popularity of some of these titles, newer accounts of the genre seem to find it difficult to regard them as part of the Hollywood musical's evolution. Some fans and critics have even been reluctant to consider some items in the sample list above as "Hollywood musicals."[2] Certainly, there have been attempts to address the post-1960s musical. Barry Keith Grant's 2012 study included a substantial number of post-classical examples as part of his overview.[3] Desirée J. Garcia unearthed the influence of the folk musical on some recent mainstream features.[4] Kelly Kessler noted how the cracks in the genre's surface between 1966 and 1983 could be read as innovations and new beginnings. But smooth integration into the canon is not always easy.[5] Sean Griffith's 2015 major overview of the genre's history, *Free and Easy?*, starts by defending an open, inclusive delimitation, and name-checks most of the aforementioned TV series, but comparatively little space is devoted to the genre's post-1980s history, comprising thirty-five years.[6] It might seem difficult to argue against this decision: not only have there been fewer musicals since the 1980s, but, in terms of sheer fun, the riches of pop-infused musicals seem to pale in comparison with the golden years at Warner Brothers or MGM. On the other hand, given the power of popular music comes partly from its specific relationship to our lives as individuals in communities, it needs to be acknowledged that the kinds of music which are culturally relevant today, belong to a tradition which is different to art songs, jazz, Tin Pan Alley, or showtunes. The new musical naturally engages with newer facets of popular music. As Dave Kehr put it in 1984: "It is pointless to ask the musical to return to other eras and styles. Whether rock is musically superior to the Tin Pan Alley tunes of the thirties and the forties is not the point."[7] Although this superiority was assumed in 1984, it would soon become clear that the issue was not so much of "quality" but of premise: maybe in looking at post-classical musicals, we need different expectations, and maybe, as it's true with other post-classical genres, the frameworks for analysis need to take into account changes in the industry and in the audience.

There is no doubt that the Hollywood musical went through important changes in the 1970s, and—as this book will argue—besides the undeniable issues of quantity, there were qualitative drivers for such shifts.[8] The contemporary film industry cannot support keeping by a stable of singers and dancers, less so a whole studio infrastructure such as the Freed Unit at MGM. But beyond that, some fans voice suspicions that the current instances of popular music are less than ideal to achieve the balance between spectacle and storytelling characteristic of the earlier phase. For traditional genre audiences, the increased use of pop music was one of the reasons the new musicals were disappointing, just as pop music listeners found the style and structure of the Broadway-based musical unexciting.[9] It is perhaps the right moment to go back to definitions of the musical in its classical manifestations and study how the new pop-influenced examples fit into these frameworks. Do both types of musical work in the same way, deal with the same topics? Clearly the new styles can be accommodated by new perspectives on the genre, but are differences more important than continuities? How about the genre's aesthetics? The present volume aims to re-assess genre developments, taking as its focus point its engagement with pop music.

I'll offer a stronger definition of what I understand by *pop music* later in this introduction. However, for the moment let me narrow down my premise: I propose that the dynamics, uses, and meanings of pop music since the 1960s have had an impact on the evolution of key content and structural tropes in the musical genre and its audiences. My project is therefore parallel to Kessler's in vindicating some of the more critically reviled aspects of post-1970s Hollywood musicals, but focuses on the impact of the development of pop music since 1955 through to 2019. The evolution of the pop music industry and popular music styles may provide us with analytic and historical tools that help us understand shifts in the themes, narration, aesthetics, and spectatorship of the newer musicals. In what follows, I argue that the shift in the music industry that took place during the mid-1950s shook the musical genre's key foundations. A great deal has been written on how pop music somehow makes the musical less rich, less interesting. Dave Kehr, in the 1984 article quoted above, suggested this might be true.[10] I am concerned with the rather different issue of how pop music makes a generative contribution to the genre. "Pop" is what audiences preferred their music to be at the same time that the musical genre began to lose its centrality. And pop music styles carry the meanings that establish links between narrative and personal experience. By using pop music as the defining matrix of many of the most important instances of the musical in the last forty years, I hope to be able to assess the ways in which the latter genre has evolved. What changes are brought in by the use of these new musical styles, how does it affect the genre, and what kind of relationship with audiences do they imply, and especially how do these "pop" musicals belong organically to the genre we know as the "Hollywood musical?" These questions provide the focus for the following chapters.

Popular Music, Rock 'n' Roll, Pop Music

The title of this volume suggests that "pop," as an adjective, will somehow qualify the evolution of the musical and its key elements. The implication is that pop-based musicals will be sufficiently different from non-pop-based musicals to earn specific attention. Consequently, this proposal puts a lot of weight on the power of the music we call "pop" to effect those changes. This section argues the distinctiveness of pop as a prelude to pursuing the issue of how pop could alter key semantic and syntactic elements of the Hollywood musical. On the other hand, and for the sake of clarity, I also need to articulate a definition of "pop music," my chosen category, as something different from overlapping labels such as "rock," "rock and roll," "popular music," and their endless subdivisions, used by other authors engaging with a similar corpus of films.

To start with, "pop music" will be discussed as something distinct from "popular music." While all pop music is popular music (i.e., subject to market dynamics, experienced and enjoyed by very broad, non-specialized audiences), not all historical forms of popular music will be considered "pop" in the following chapters. Donald Clarke, in *The Rise and Fall of Popular Music*, seems to trace the decadence of American popular music to the mid-1950s: the same period when "pop music," in the sense used in this volume, became central.[11] For Clarke, "good" popular music peaked around the swing era, driven by radio, dance orchestras, the Broadway musical, and popular jazz performers. Popular songs were tailored to follow certain conventions of melody, meter, and structure that made them quickly memorable.[12] Some of this effect was by design, for example, successful producers like Berry Gordy at Motown would insist that every song meet certain standards to ensure its playability.[13]

Cole Porter and Frank Sinatra were, and continue to be, popular music, even if they were increasingly perceived as different (in terms of market, in terms of meanings and aesthetics) from Elvis, the Beach Boys, or the Beatles. The older generation also felt threatened by the newer approaches. During the rise of pop music in the 1950s, at the peak of the Broadway showtune, pop lyrics, structures, and melodies seemed to some more repetitive, simplistic, and uncouth: Sinatra, Richard Rodgers, and Oscar Hammerstein were among the artists who expressed their distaste for the new forms. But, as pointed out by leading scholars like Simon Frith, pop songs were not just about certain uses of melody or rhythm. There was a whole social context tied to their aesthetics, and pop music cannot be understood without reference to this context.

Identifying "pop" music as distinctive and different from previous models entails considering the industrial context for the change and justifying, as Richard A. Peterson does in a key article, why exactly there was a change of paradigm in popular music in the mid-1950s.[14] Major record companies such as RCA, Decca, and Columbia had dominated the jazz and showtunes business for three decades. Smaller companies, such as Sun Records, were supporting new performers and producing new kinds of songs which caught the attention of a young audience; their being smaller companies, with lower stakes, helped this process of innovation, and their success changed the map of the music industry. The entity managing music rights in America for the early years of recorded music for radio broadcast was the American Society of Composers, Authors, and Publishers (ASCAP), which counted among its members the great majority of mainstream music artists. A competing, lower-stakes association, Broadcast Music, Inc. (BMI), was created in 1939. ASCAP retained power on what was played by most radio stations, whereas BMI's catalogue included the kind of items and performers that ASCAP did not handle as they were considered less profitable. The latter included, crucially, Black performers and songwriters. As Peterson's account details, the 1950s saw newer, smaller radio companies licensed. Unable or unwilling to pay the high ASCAP fees, most made agreements with BMI to broadcast their artists. This situation gave airtime to a whole repertoire of music that had been seldom heard in mainstream institutions until then. The BMI catalogue included many Black singers that did not fit into the ASCAP product. "Race," and also "country," were two such categories. "Race" music was, simply, music made by Black artists, inspired by Black experience and traditions, and marketed at a Black audience. By 1947, the derogatory term changed to "rhythm and blues" (R & B) and had its own charts. Some of it sounded very much like what would be called "rock and roll" ten years later, although some critics have insisted that it wasn't until rock and roll was taken up by white singers that it had an impact on the mainstream.[15]

This is the music that inspired the work of many white early rockers, including Elvis Presley, Jerry Lee Lewis, and Buddy Holly. "Rock and roll," the first wave of the new pop music, appeared then as a label which certainly seemed to be new to the mainstream, but its success has to be understood along social lines: white appropriation of Black music, marketing youth lifestyles, and encouraging teen consumerism. This suggests that, along with a certain sound and the industrial context sketched out above, the third area in which the new pop music was distinctive was the social base it addressed. The rise of pop implied a new relationship between its listeners and the music business, and this new relationship would have an impact on the content and uses of popular music.[16] The history of pop music is not just the history of successive companies and styles, but also the history of its meaning in the context of social identities and structures of feeling: beyond the actual music, it takes into account the way it created attitudes, fantasies, politics, listening communities. This accounts for the fact that most pop songs in the genre's infancy were about a limited range of themes, which might be irrelevant after leaving the enchanted kingdom of teenageland: proms, faithless boyfriends, flowing tears, eternal love, surf, cars, parties. But in sinking its roots into communities, the implications of pop would change as those communities evolved.

One justification for discussing rock and roll and other post-1955 varieties of pop music together, is the way both are capable of articulating social or personal issues in a language that is understood by consumers. According to Simon Frith's sociology-based approach, pop music started as youth music: it thrived as a business under the premise that youngsters would consume new music to a greater extent than adults and therefore it would be a good idea to target them as ideal buyers.[17] Ian Chambers summarizes the shift in the following terms:

> It is tempting to see in the change of terminology from "popular" to "pop" that occurred in the mid-1950s a simple historical divide between the field of commercial popular music in general and a more precise area associated with a "teenage" public. But the abbreviation of the term involved more than a purely generational division in taste. It also suggested a precise musical and cultural shift. The voices of Little Richard and Elvis Presley came out of a musical tradition quite different from that of Frank Sinatra, Rosemary Clooney and the other doyens of post-war American popular music. This sonorial clash lies behind much of the subsequent history of popular music and the arrival of pop as a distinctive sound.[18]

Pop music also was endowed with a ritualistic, identity-creating element that challenged equivalent rituals associated with previously mainstream music. Buying the Beatles' records is not just a matter of personal preference: taste works as social discourse, as Pierre Bourdieu describes, which then has an impact on who we are and our place in the community.[19] For Dick Hebdige, pop music is one of the key drivers of subculture.[20] These elements made pop music extraordinarily successful, but also slightly incompatible, at least at the beginning, with the kinds of stories featured in mainstream movies of the 1960s.

These perspectives account for the broad agreement about 1955 as a watershed point: this is the year in which rock and roll became a distinct cultural entity. The new label is the first, the most lasting, and most densely mythologized of the pop music trends. Stylistically, the new music was a hybrid that incorporated different elements from folk, country, and blues with other genres of Black music. In contrast to the gentle swing and vocal styles that relied on the lyrics, even in jazz, the new sounds were described by critics as shouts, yells, and roars. In a way, it is easier to describe rock's style negatively—to describe what it wasn't. The attitudes to rock were oppositional:[21] it was the music of the teenage rebellion.[22] As a consequence, rock and roll had to be whatever the old styles of popular music were not: it claimed to be unsophisticated, untidy, visceral. Then again, the mix was not stable: different strands would come to dominate, expand, and eventually produce new alternative paths. The cross-influences were so dense, particularly from the mid-sixties, that we could also argue that rock and roll was firstly a mythology and only secondly a particular style of music. As a mythology it has survived into the twenty-first century, even if the original rock and roll "sound" has been consigned to nostalgic recuperations.[23] In fact, the meaning of rock and roll and later forms of pop music has always been tied up to their power to create mythologies which appealed to different groups, as opposed to the fantasy of a popular music addressing "everybody." Pop music styles outside of rock and roll are similarly characterized by their historical roots: doo wop, for instance, evolved from Black kids creating small scale gospel-influenced chorales on street corners. These roots, these histories, can become activated in rock and roll–related narratives and throughout this book we'll often come back to the way narratives in pop musicals feature aspects of pop music history.

And, of course, new sounds emerged as new contexts did. Instrumentation changed and became more open to new technologies, electric guitars later became a typical marker of many (not all) rock styles, and there tended to be more emphasis on rhythm, less emphasis on lyrics, and a distinctly new approach to vocal articulation. Often the songs also started from different premises and dealt with musical and lyrical content in different ways: the range of aesthetic frameworks in the new pop songs was broader than it was in the older popular music, sometimes resembling old Tin Pan Alley conventions. In some accounts, distinctions between pop and "rock and roll" are blurred: Marshall Crenshaw's guide, *Hollywood Rock,* includes a variety of films featuring soundtracks of many pop genres,[24] as is also the case with David L. James's academic *Rock 'n' Film*. "Rock and roll" was the name given to the style that emerged in 1954, first manifested by Black singers such as Little Richard but fixed in commercial terms by whites like Bill Haley and Elvis Presley. Rock and roll was one of the key signifiers of change in the mid-1950s: it meant "sex," it meant "not your daddy's music," it would soon come to mean "authenticity" against the perceived phoniness of crooners and Broadway singers. For

Bob Stanley, "the beauty of rock 'n' roll was not just its newness but its gleeful awareness of its newness, wiping out the repression of the post war decade." Frith adds: "Rock was the last romantic attempt to preserve ways of music making—performer as artist, performance as community—that had been made obsolete by technology and capital."[25] Future incarnations of rock and roll preserved the rebelliousness and the attitude: sometimes this was heartfelt, sometimes it was a marketing tool.[26]

But pop music, as defined in this volume, encompasses additional styles to rock and roll. In his overview, Tim Wall critiques the "rock-based" history of popular music that gave undue prominence to rock and roll and measured many contributions based on their ability to be like rock.[27] The second wave of rock and rollers in the late sixties would be labeled simply "rock" music, and despite the diversity of rock styles by then, they all preserved and developed the attitudes of early rock and roll and the articulation of a discourse about the generation gap. Although the Beatles, who toured the United States for the first time in 1964, are considered the keepers of the tradition, it would be other groups like the Rolling Stones, the Who, and the Doors who would keep the rock mythologies alive as the 1960s progressed. Rock claimed to reject commercialism and presented itself in terms of authenticity—a key aspect of rock mythology which for some distinguishes it from other pop forms. If we regard pop music as an industry and a general approach to a listening audience, rock is something closer to a mystique. By the late sixties, "authentic" rock was one of the languages of the counterculture: no matter what the songs said, rock was always about the youthful aspiration for change and the rejection of conservative attitudes towards rock, education, class, drugs, and sexuality.[28]

Although many books on pop music and film prefer the label "rock musicals" to the one chosen for this volume, I think that the former is restrictive for imposing a certain rock approach on a very broad range of styles. The scores of *Bikini Beach*, *Saturday Night Fever* (1977), *Can't Stop the Music* (1980), *Moulin Rouge!*, *Dreamgirls*, *Little Shop of Horrors*, *Grease*, *Dirty Dancing*, and *Wild Style* are inspired by different pop music styles, often with very little "rock" in them, and these styles affect the films in different ways; *The Rocky Horror Picture Show*, *The Blues Brothers*, *Rock and Roll High School*, *Sid and Nancy* (1986), *Rent* (2005), *Rock of Ages* (2012), and *Hedwig and the Angry Inch* (2001) have more specifically rock-driven scores. By the 1970s, pop had diversified. Sometimes it was even combined with non-pop styles: many rock-based scores, like *Jesus Christ Superstar* (1973), add in some softer pop ballads or even traditional showtunes. Maintaining the purity of rock mythology was a delicate balancing act between "authenticity" and "spectacle," and films would struggle to engage with this tension. Then again, in looking at rock as a performance, a pose, a mythology, rather than taking its authenticity literally, it becomes just one of the masks of the overall multifaceted phenomenon of pop music. All mythologies are untrue, even those that claim "authenticity." Even if gatekeepers will insist on sharp differences, slippages between rock and pop are—and were—common. And rock ethos being so specific, it is often too limited to be able to deal with plot or characterization. In the scope of this book, rock and its mythologies have a place within the dynamics of pop music, rather than being sharply opposed to them.

The label "pop" is used, and preferred, in this book as an inclusive category which, agreeing with Bob Stanley's definition:

> includes rock, R&B, soul, hip hop, house, techno, metal and country. If you make records, singles and albums, and if you go on TV or on tour to promote them, you're in the pop business. If you sing a cappella folk songs in a pub in Whitby, you're not. Pop needs an audience that the artist doesn't know personally—it has to be transferable. Most basically, anything that gets into the charts is pop, be it Buddy Holly, Black Sabbath or Bucks Fizz.[29]

Although his account includes instances of the "old" popular music, Stanley chooses one hard criterion for his definition of pop: the introduction of official pop charts in the music press. Charts have been the backbone of the popular music industry since the 1950s. It is a hard criterion that homogenizes audiences, styles, and mythologies, turning them into a number. At the same time, it emphasizes the new logic that separates "popular music" from "pop music."

Each of the styles listed by Stanley lends itself to different connotations when performed. Some of these styles became prominent in the movies. Doo wop, for example, originating as a Black folk style, one that was raw but effective, developed into a tame version of teen music that insisted on elegance and technique; and instances of this style can be heard in *Jersey Boys* (2014) and, of course, in *Grease*. Motown, although not politically confrontational, could not avoid engaging with race in a decade that saw violent civil rights struggles. The sound characterizes a period, and is used in *Dreamgirls* and *The Wiz* (1978), whereas the girl-group sound is used by Alan Menken both in *Little Shop of Horrors* and *Hercules*. Surf music would bring to the fore memories of teen utopia, particularly in the AIP "beach party" cycle of films but also later in films like *Grease* or *The Teen Beach Movie* (2013). Glam rock, an offshoot of rock and roll, is used in Haynes's *Velvet Goldmine*, whereas the strongly anti-commercial, anti-assimilation punk is featured, among other musical styles, in *Hedwig and the Angry Inch* and in *Sid and Nancy*. Disco's connotations, both erotic and social, are well articulated in *Saturday Night Fever*, *Thank God It's Friday!*, (1978) and *Can't Stop the Music*.[30] Of course, hip-hop—which for some practitioners is more of a "folk" than a "pop" style of music—is featured in a number of biopics. These include the TV series *The Get Down* and *Empire*, and feature film *8 Mile*, as well as the break dancing cycle of the early 1980s, which highlighted issues of race and the experience of living on the margins of the system. Soul, which reflects a Black experience, is heard in *What's Love Got to Do with It* and in Effie's stylings in *Dreamgirls*, where it is semantically opposed to the more mainstream Motown sound.[31]

To sum up, pop, and rock as a particular strand within it, are forms of commercial music which reflect cultural attitudes and are addressed to various interpretive communities. Pop music was born as youth music and developed in a variety of ways to include the poetic, the social, and even the philosophical. In addition to these new directions, rock carries with it a very specific mythology that includes a rejection of commercialism, a bid for authenticity, and a disgust for bourgeois society. For the purposes of this book, I will be interrogating the Hollywood musical from the perspective of the broader label "pop." From this contextualization, it becomes apparent that there is a certain lack of synchronicity between the criteria required to attain this label, and the conventions of the traditional Hollywood musical. But by the 1970s, we find more complex negotiations between pop music and the musical. The next section is about the changes that embracing pop music and its cultural implications brought to Hollywood.

Pop and the Musical: Tensions and Synergies

A definition of the "pop musical" is inevitably linked to general proposals on what constitutes a musical. Complex accounts of the genre exist at least since Rick Altman discussed the musical from the perspective of literary genre theory in 1987 and proposed a regularly referred to set of traits and categories. Altman proposed three types of musical—the fairy tale, the backstage and the folk musical—according to a set of content-based and structural criteria (figures 0.1–0.3). By contrast, when faced with a similar challenge many years later for his account of the American musical, Sean Griffin opted for a looser, delimiting, approach to what constitutes a musical.[32] In popular culture, no rigorous characterization that accounts for a genre label can resist fifty years of challenges, and the canon Griffin studied was less consistent than the titles that illustrated Altman's proposals: since the 1970s the classical genre's repertoire has been questioned both from the outside (critics and audiences finding them predictable or conservative) and from the inside (artists producing self-reflexive or self-questioning instances of genre). Griffin gave up on providing a very narrow definition of the genre, and instead included what he considered new manifestations of the musical, whose status would have been questioned by previous scholars and fans.[33]

Fig. 0.1: Fairy-tale musical. *Dirty Dancing*.

Fig. 0.2: Backstage musical. *Dreamgirls*.

Fig. 0.3: Folk musical. *Mamma Mia!*

Other debates on the framework for defining the post-1970s musical, such as Feuer's argument about the implications of considering *Dirty Dancing* a musical or Dyer's provocative chapter on *Car Wash* (1976), suggest to me the essential impossibility of providing a narrow definition: something clear and with a set of stable criteria that can be applied both to classical and post-classical musicals.[34] The same hesitations can be felt when selecting representative examples, as evident in the selection of essays that make up the 2017 volume *Contemporary Musical Film*, which include examples like *The Fast and the Furious* (2001) and *Kill Bill: Vol. 1 & 2* (2003, 2004) that are certainly "musical films," but cannot fit into any satisfactory definition of "a musical."[35] Like Griffin, Feuer, and

Dyer, I would argue that we need to adapt our characterization of the musical to new instances, rather than exclude them if they don't fulfill traditional definitions. Looking at the post-1970s titles listed earlier in this introduction, I note how established two tropes in particular seem (despite some notable exceptions): a romantic couple who remain central throughout the narrative, and dance used for courting purposes or to celebrate community. In the contemporary age, this is less common: music can now do other things besides bringing lovers together. Some of this evolution is the result of the musical absorbing certain elements (mythologies, sounds, biographies) of pop music, but some of the changes are more generally based on the erosion of the genre system that took place in the 1970s. In my discussion of relevant examples, I am concerned both with the originality of the pop musical and also with continuities between the post-1970s titles and the classical musicals as sampled in accounts by Hirschhorn and Kobal, or Altman, Babington, and Evans, etc.

In order to distinguish it from "a musical *film*," "a musical," in the context of this book, is a narrative form of fiction film (that is, not a videoclip, a filmed concert or a documentary, no matter how important these forms have been in shaping the current manifestations of the musical genre), that uses diegetic song or dance (or both) in a sustained way; song and dance must contribute to the story layers of meaning that would be absent otherwise. The more central musical moments (in the form of song and dance) are to the story, the more central the film will be to the discussion. Narrative is therefore quite central to my definition, as indeed it is both for those who have grappled with delimitations, such as Altman, Feuer, or Bill Marshall and Robyn Stilwell, and for those who deal more generally with the power of cinema as a basically narrative medium.[36] It is another of this book's premises that pop music had an impact on both the semantic and the syntactic elements of traditional musicals as described by Altman, contributing to the destabilization of the relatively stable genre patterns he identifies.

What follows is a highly selective outline of the major and minor changes to the genre produced by pop's impact, that does not attempt to discuss every constituting element of the Hollywood musical, but simply uses some of the genre's key aspects to suggest ways in which the gravitational force of pop music—as an industry and as a mythology—affected established conventions. I use traits recurring in key accounts of the musical genre, and illustrate ways in which they are recontextualized in films using pop music substantially. Some of them will be developed further in the examples, others, inevitably, less so. All of them are featured in the body of films that fall under the "pop musical" label.

Let's start our brief overview of pop's impact on the musical, with a recurring characterization in scholarship of the musical as folk art. Desirée J. Garcia highlights continuities in the way the folk musical has transformed itself over the decades.[37] But this can be complemented with the different inflections brought on by a consideration of certain pop music styles as folk. More generally, Feuer discusses the genre's relationship (contradictory, paradoxical) to "folk" art: folk here is not a type of music but an attitude to certain music genres.[38] For Feuer, elements of "spontaneous" folk art are displayed to conceal what was really a well-oiled production and marketing machinery. In her 2017 study, *Hip Hop on Film*, Kimberley Monteyne develops this idea, testing it against the short cycle of break dancing musicals of the early 1980s and finds a front of evolution that keeps some essential structural themes but brings to the fore a host of social issues on life in America's inner cities.[39] Here, folk art means something more specifically tied to *social* realities. Rather than just being something characters do (break dancing or graffiti) to set a scene, folk art can have a substantial ideological impact on the narrative. If many pop musicals with roots in street culture can still be considered "folk," the social implications of this 1980s cycle are now inescapable. The new "folk" engages directly with class, race, history, and gender, as examples in chapter 4 will bear out. And the effort it takes to produce musical performance tends to be exhibited rather than concealed: Charlie Ahearn's *Wild Style* expresses this effort not just in its plot, but also in the way it presents itself almost as a "guerilla" film with deep roots in the community. The very nature of some socially aware pop styles has brought up a new awareness for the social. As a telling metaphor, sweat—a taboo in classical musicals, as it was a sign of effort—is palpable in *Dirty Dancing*, *Hedwig*, *Fame*, and *Step Up*.[40] The new "folk" are far from happy peasants who find art "natural": in these instances they have to sweat to express themselves.

Besides its status as folk art, the musical has also been frequently discussed in terms of its utopian values. Related to the concealment of effort, the central notion of popular music's utopian enticements is still

Fig. 0.4: Sun-kissed utopia: *Teen Beach Movie* (2013).

evident in films like *Teen Beach Movie* (figure 0.4), *Saturday Night Fever*, *Velvet Goldmine*, and *Hedwig and the Angry Inch*, but now it comes with a twist: none of these films embrace utopia as wholeheartedly as previous examples. This is consistent in the new musicals. Even Richard Dyer, the key proponent of the utopian qualities of mainstream entertainment, writing in 1977, would come to ask himself a key question: "Utopia for whom?"[41] Again, the pop musical acknowledges the idea that some people's utopias arise out of somebody else's oppression. The plots of the above four examples openly acknowledge this idea of gain and loss, with an emphasis on the latter.

Specific semantic elements of the musical genre may have different implications when framed by pop music. Let's consider the most characteristic location for the genre's plot in its classical manifestations. One of the key settings of the Hollywood musical is the stage, and its reconfiguration into the pop concert venue has an impact on the relationship between musical numbers and diegetic audiences. The stage in traditional musicals tends to be clearly framed, often draped in red curtains, establishing a hard border between performers and their spectators, and the mise en scène of musical numbers taking place on that stage reinforces that hard border (see an example from *Easter Parade* [1948], figures 0.5–0.6).

Fig. 0.5: The view from the stage. *Easter Parade*.

Fig. 0.6: The view from the audience. *Easter Parade*.

Feuer's characterization of the genre is very dependent on the symbolic force of that border, the axis that marks dynamics between performers and their audience.[42] The conception here is that of eighteenth-century theatre and opera, which carries implications of a certain bourgeois approach to entertainment, with tidy rows of well-behaved, often well-dressed audiences, quietly appreciative of the performance who applaud right on cue, so different from the forms favored by cheering, often screaming young audiences as represented in *Bye Bye Birdie* (1963) or *A Hard Day's Night* (1964).

As Feuer and others theorizing the genre remark, this hard border is effectively made explicit in the mise en scène. Although the stage continues to be one key semantic element in pop musicals, the pop stage brings to mind different connotations: it tends to be more open, less organized, it works less to isolate performers from audiences (characters may cross the stage frame into the space of the audience, as in *Dirty Dancing*, see figures 0.7 and 0.8). Diegetic break dancing street performances in *Beat Street* (figures 0.9), *Breakin'* (1984), and *Delivery Boys* (1985) take place on the slightest hint of a stage. Characters in *The Rose* (1979), *Velvet Goldmine*, *Rocketman* (2019), and *Straight Outta Compton* also seem to have a more fluid relationship with their audiences than in, say, *Gold Diggers of 1933* (1933), *Top Hat* (1935), or *Easter Parade* where, despite reaction shots, the stage is presented as an independent space. *The Rocky Horror Picture Show* ends with a stage show, which is interrupted as rebellious aliens with laser guns decide the party's over. One character appears to be shot dead on stage in *Velvet Goldmine*, and a gun is kicked from backstage to the stage and into the audience in *Moulin Rouge!*. Performers tend to be filmed surrounded by an audience, rather than away from them, as in *Velvet Goldmine*, *The Rose*, and *Rocketman* (figure 0.10).

What's more, the very concept of a "stage," the area where the music is performed, is diversified in order to naturalize the music sources: the recording studio is now one of the key sites for pop musicals, starting with *Jailhouse Rock* (1957) and including *American Hot Wax* (1978), *Dreamgirls*, *Nashville*, *Bohemian Rhapsody* (2018), *A Star is Born* (2018), *Velvet Goldmine* (figure 0.11), and *The Buddy Holly Story* (1978), as well as the TV series *Empire*. Another approach to the performance area is represented by the TV studio set. And, as in the case of the pop concert stage, the distance between a TV broadcast and the living room is bridged successfully

Fig. 0.7: Crossing the stage frame. *Dirty Dancing*.

Fig. 0.8: The audience become performers. *Dirty Dancing*.

in *Hairspray* and in *Bye Bye Birdie*. This all suggests a re-signification of the strong image of the stage in the musical that has affected its syntax. If the trope of a fixed dynamic between onstage and offstage is central for traditional musicals, in more recent examples we see this tension becoming softer and less conventional.

Fig. 0.9: Barely a stage. *Beat Street*.

Fig. 0.10: The performer and the audience. *Rocketman*.

Other tropes central to the musical have experienced interesting evolutions. Musical numbers used to be predicated on a limited repertoire of ideas surrounding the body, cultural identity, sexuality, and gender, which are later presented in more complex, challenging ways. All four of these themes have had long traditions of representation. Let's start with the physical body and its role in the classical musical. Bodies are prominently featured in 1930s Busby Berkley musicals and occasionally later. Still, in these instances the focus is on the energy the actors' bodies generate

Fig. 0.11: The recording studio. *Velvet Goldmine*.

rather than the body's materiality per se. In pop musicals, fleshy, heavy bodies are present in their physicality. The image of sweat is, again, a good illustration of this shift. Furthermore, writing on disco in 1979, Richard Dyer remarks on the way disco dancing had a strong focus on the whole body.[43] With some exceptions, bodies in classical musicals tend to be composed and elegant. Leading men and leading ladies keep their heads erect and only comedians are pointedly awkward in their bearing. Women's bodies are wrapped in spectacular dresses, and the wrapping draws most of the attention: costuming is one of the film elements we most frequently associate with the classical musical. And in good heterosexual fashion, it is women, not men, that are the object of a voyeuristic gaze. True, there are the semi-naked chorus boys in Jack Cole's "Ain't There Anyone Here for Love" from *Gentlemen Prefer Blondes* (1953), but these were not part of a trend. Newer dancing styles, as in *Fame* or *The Wiz*, are less tidy, less organized, and provide an image of the body which becomes more real, heavier, with men displaying flesh and sweat and presented as sexual objects.

Secondly, identity, as Altman demonstrates, is continually *performed* in musicals, but it has also been limited to certain notions of America[44] and to stereotypes that have moral implications. Hollywood musicals, particularly those Altman labels "folk musicals," have frequently produced a consistent, monolithic, view of America. No matter what musicals meant for individuals, orthodox ideologies of nation, ethnicity, and sexuality were often imposed. In particular, as many studies have shown, race was restricted to a handful of stereotypes.[45] The cultural revolutions of the 1960s drove the change to the idea of an "American" identity and that in turn affected the premises of the genre. Musicals that attempted a nostalgic, luminous view of a white America were seen as reactionary. Pop music was one of the cultural sites where official identities were reconsidered. And alternative identities, contradictory and struggling, could be given a voice. From then on, a range of ethnic and cultural identities were systematically performed and even challenged. Newer musicals featured aspects of American cultural history determined by race and politics: *Hair*, *Hairspray*, and others are critical about aspects of American identity. As if trying to pay an old debt, ethnicity becomes, particularly from the 1980s, a key theme of the pop musical, being politically developed in *Hairspray* (figure 0.12) and *Zoot Suit* (1981), but also articulated in *Dreamgirls*, the hip-hop cycle, and *Save the Last Dance* (2001).

Thirdly, explicit sexuality was largely a taboo subject until the 1970s, and even more so in musicals, where an idealized heterosexual harmony replaced any realistic approach to gender tensions, repression, or desire. And even if scholars have identified challenges to the heterosexual dynamics in the Hollywood musical, finding female characters with stronger voices and agency, and gay creative talent who are agents of narrative and performance,[46] the fact is that, again, representation depended on

Fig. 0.12: They know where they've been. Politics in *Hairspray*.

stereotyping all sexual dissenters. Fourthly, and finally, the pop musical also presents new approaches to gender. The counterculture, feminism, and gay rights changed the way these elements were conveyed. In a world where gender conventions were imposed and fixed, and where expressions of sexuality were censored or sidestepped, clearly there was little space for the expression of gender dissidence. Pop music as an institution has developed discourses on sexuality. So pop-based musicals can't (and, more pointedly, won't) ignore sex or sexual identity, as illustrated by *The Rocky Horror Picture Show*, *Grease*, *Patient Zero* (2018), *Rent*, *Velvet Goldmine*, and *Hedwig and the Angry Inch*.

Regarding issues of *style*, pop songs have tended to replace showtunes, operetta arias, comedy songs, and character songs in post-classical musicals, and this has an impact on the range of things the musical numbers can communicate. In assessing what pop songs bring to the musical, we must consider, firstly, that a song's meaning is not conveyed only through melody, rhythm, and lyrics: engaging with an audience's memories, viewpoints, and personal background can be powerful in unleashing meaning as well. When assessing pop songs, we need to consider cultural implications as equally important to content and form. Secondly, style and content are not monolithic, and pop songs become more ambitious as the lexicon of pop styles becomes broader in the 1960s, when pop performers start quoting Rimbaud, Tolkien, and Wilde, for example (three of the main influences for glam rockers). Less theatrical than the songs created for the stage or for mature singers like Sinatra, pop songs don't attempt irony or humour or even believable heartbreak per se, but many pop musicals frame their musical numbers in such a way as to convey those qualities: "Beauty School Drop Out," from *Grease*; "Touch-A, Touch-A, Touch Me," from *The Rocky Horror Picture Show*; Madonna's "Like a Virgin" in *Moulin Rouge!*; and "I Won't Say I'm In Love," from *Hercules*, are examples of this. As Ryan Bunch suggests,[47] the pop beat of "Let It Go" in *Frozen* (2013), in contrasting with previous showtune-influenced songs and with other non-pop Disney songs, adds force and conviction to Elsa's rebellion, and, as it soon became clear, elicits a stronger emotional response from its intended audience.[48]

Traditional professional singers in the classical musical were also cultural figures, in that they represented ideals of elegance or talent that spoke confidently to their audience about themes of love or gender with a shared ideological premise. Singers in pop musicals, however, need to engage with their intended youth audience and somehow set themselves apart from prior ideologies, exploiting the more rebellious significance of their star personae. Rock, for example, encourages a particular type of singer that was unknown until the late 1950s: tough, uncouth, and rebellious.[49] This then affects the range of characterizations, which in turn inflects plot types. The "rise and fall" narratives are a correlative of a new mythology of the pop star. Most post-1970 music star biopics have their protagonists' fame and talent peaking in the film's first half, only to encounter difficulties incarnated in managers, partners, or addictions to be resolved in the rest of the film.[50] As for performance technique, it involves a different approach to the articulation of music and lyrics. In the age of operetta, singers had trained voices, and were supposed to be able to negotiate a demanding score. This conveyed certain ideas or artistry and elegance, of European sophistication, of the values of conservative approaches to art.[51] The standard Tin Pan Alley song is far less demanding, and so musicals starring Al Jolson, Alice Faye, or Ethel Merman, all effective singers, shifted focus away from elegant melodic lines and high notes towards performance and personality by emphasizing lyrical content. Pop music later brought on yet another change to the relationship between the singer and the song. First, because the demands and personae of pop singers had little to do with those of conventional actors. As a consequence, many singers without proper acting training have given excellent performances in pop musicals; Beyoncé (figure 0.13), Prince, and Ice-T are good examples of this. Second, because the pop song from the rock and roll era onwards has put less emphasis on the lyrics and has allowed for an approach to singing in which words or syntax do not need to be comprehended by audiences. The pop biopic features various relationships between the pop stars being portrayed, the star portraying them, and the "voice." Chapter 3 explores the different versions of these relationships, including actors doing their own singing (Kevin Spacey in *Beyond the Sea* [2004], Angela Basset in *What's Love Got to Do with It*, Taron Edgerton in *Rocketman*) and examples in which the singer has dubbed the performance (Jerry Lee Lewis in *Great Balls of Fire!*, Ray Charles in *Ray* [2004]).[52]

A final, related, stylistic point, which Sean Griffin raises, is important to highlight here. For many historians, post-1982 musicals are increasingly

Fig. 0.13: Beyoncé as Deena in *Dreamgirls*.

influenced by what has come to be called "MTV style." Griffin gives a clear outline of this style: his key idea is that the advent of MTV subsequently encouraged the use of loose "montage" sequences in pop musicals, and therefore editing became less narratively motivated and therefore less classical.[53] As he acknowledges, montage sequences were unknown in traditional musicals beyond some anomalous examples such as the "Wedding of the Painted Doll" in *Singin' in the Rain* (1952) and the rehearsal montage in *The Band Wagon* (1953). For Griffin, this influences the looseness in the approach to the links between numbers and plot in pop musicals. From a different perspective, Marco Calavita concludes that the influence of MTV in musicals might be less central than some propose, as the aesthetics are in fact evolving from approaches already in use by artists trained in the Hollywood/Broadway tradition, such as Bob Fosse.[54]

One syntactic change affected the very narrative spine of the genre. One of the elements in Altman's classification that from a contemporary perspective, signals a sharp change in the evolution of the genre is the traditional musical's absolute emphasis on courtship: the heterosexual couple as the driving force of every musical, the best manifestation of its double focus structure. As the range of films selected here will attest, there are less and less post-1970 musicals, whether pop or not, that put heterosexual couples at their centre. Musicals, even when they feature couples, put their energies into other projects: identity, nostalgia, satire, or history, for instance. Even with those cases that feature couples, the ending does not always suggest the kind of "happily ever after" that one assumes in

Fred and Ginger musicals. Dual focus is at the heart of the genre for Altman. Many pop musicals continue to establish the tension between opposites through a couple: *Moulin Rouge!*, *Little Shop of Horrors*, *Grease*, *Hairspray*, *Dirty Dancing*. But courting loses its previous centrality, as *Jesus Christ Superstar*, *Tommy* (1975), *Dreamgirls*, *The Rocky Horror Picture Show*, *Beat Street*, *Can't Stop the Music*, and *Straight Outta Compton* all demonstrate. And some musicals even end with a break-up or death rather than a confirmation of the heterosexual couple: *What's Love Got to Do with It*, *Dreamgirls*, *Ray*, *The Rose*, *Moulin Rouge!*, and *Hedwig* all conclude this way. *Saturday Night Fever* ends with rape, and a suggestion that, despite this nasty moment, the main couple might end up being "just friends." One way to explain this trend towards a decentralization of courting is that, in a context where sex can be represented as sex, no "Night and Day" or "Dancing in the Dark" is required to suggest sexual attraction: at the end of *Grease*, sexual attraction is represented in the musical number "You're the One That I Want" simply as, well, sexual. And unhappy endings are more acceptable since the 1970s than they used to be. It is not uncommon for relationships to end in tears, although it is particularly striking that so many musical relationships do, given the genre's investment in representing happiness.

No review of key syntactic differences between the musical as conceived in traditional practices and the pop musical can ignore the issue of integration.[55] "Integration" is the approach a musical takes to the relationship between its numbers and its plot, often consisting of reinforcing plot points or character traits through song. In many non-integrated musicals, there is a clear alternation between the musical numbers and plot, with musical numbers generally following a logic of attractions. Integration proposes that the songs need to engage more tightly with the plot (advancing the story), characters (communicating their traits, desires, and choices), or narrative context (evoking a sense of place, time, or the customs of the musical's location). Although it is one of the recurring motifs and will be unpacked further in the three chapters that follow, let us here note that there was a historical shift in the way integration worked. Integration is not fundamental to the musical, but neither can it be completely dismissed. At the very least, the pop musical suggests a reconfiguration in the relationship between musical numbers and plot. Pop musicals were born when a certain type of Broadway show was at its peak, with formulae well in place;

it somehow represented another pathway into cinematic uses of popular music. It needs to be said that integration has not always been central to the Hollywood musical. Early film musicals tended towards the revue format, and the Warner Brothers' cycle tended to have musical numbers exist in a separate stage world, sometimes pushing some of them all together towards the end of the film. On the other hand, certain important Broadway shows from the 1920s onwards and, particularly, after the success of *Oklahoma!* in 1943, created the notion that integration was superior to non-integration. No matter how many examples there were to the contrary, there was a mystique to integration which was not too different in impact to the Wagnerian revolution in opera. With the rise of pop music in the 1950s, that mystique was at its height and had wormed its way into the conscience of fans of the musical as a genre. Since the 1940s, some kind of relationship between song and plot was expected for musicals to be taken seriously, and those which did not attempt that, as was the case with the Latin-flavored Carmen Miranda cycle at Fox, were simply seen as less respectable. Joseph Andrew Casper discusses at length in his book on Vincent Minnelli,[56] how full Broadway-style integration in Minnelli's 1940s musicals at MGM was identified with "quality." By the 1950s this idea had taken hold.

Ask many fans and even critics what integration is all about and the reply will be something along the lines of, "songs must contribute to the plot," meaning that during the musical number, ideally, something must happen to propel the plot forward. But musical numbers or songs can carry out a number of functions other than to "contribute to the plot." As Richard Dyer argues in *In the Space of a Song*, sometimes they simply characterize or set up an atmosphere. And in most instances the decorative uses of song and dance far exceed their plot relevance. In an important essay, *The Musical as Drama*, McMillin dissects the concept of integration and concludes that its centrality has been more theoretical than practical; it has been more focused on certain moments of certain shows than existing throughout the genre as a constant.[57] In other words, many musical numbers in Broadway and, by extension, Hollywood integrated musicals, are not "integrated" at all unless the notion is expanded to include a wider range of relationships between plot and musical numbers. As McMillin, Kessler, and John Mueller suggest from complementary perspectives,[58] we need to revisit the concept to include, for instance, the numbers in the Warner Brothers' Busby Berkeley cycle. I will engage with integration further in chapter 2, by suggesting that the new approaches contributed by pop styles encourage a broader view of integration that goes beyond the old adage, "when emotions become too intense, characters sing." Together with the scholars mentioned previously, I believe the uses of integration in the pop musical can bring out different relationships between music and narrative.[59]

In this broad sense, even dance musicals such as *Saturday Night Fever*, *Wild Style*, *Beat Street*, *Dirty Dancing*, the *Step Up* films, and *Save the Last Dance* would be considered "integrated," despite containing songs or themes unrelated to plot points or characterization and seldom having characters actually sing the songs. Rather than dismissing the term completely, due to the inconsistent way it can be used, I have opted for using its rich history to test it and adapt it to the pop musical. The challenge of integration in the pop musical does not come so much from enabling songs to be smoothly integrated with plot and characters, but from using certain aspects of the songs, their style, and the mythologies they evoke, to work within longer structures. Although we need to keep on looking into the relationship between musical numbers and a film's overall meaning, we also need to accept that such a relationship will not always be literal and contribute to the "plot." Some numbers in the Elvis films, in the AIP beach party series, even in *Help!* (1965) and *Yellow Submarine* (1968), are integrated into their plot even if conceived, as it is the case with many traditional musicals, for a different context. But then again it seems that pop musical conventions allow for musical numbers that are less specific to plot situations.

This Book

This book addresses the way pop music, its performance, its stars, and its history became a hugely influential line of development for the post-1970 Hollywood musical, bringing in a shift that would affect the genre's premises. It will discuss only narrative feature films, excluding the rock/pop concert film (a subgenre with its own dynamics that became central to the relationships between film and pop music). Also, although examples from British pop musicals will be used for the sake of comparison, and many of the examples considered have their origin in Britain or are specifically related to British musical cultures (*The Rocky Horror Picture Show*, *Rocketman*, *Velvet Goldmine*), the focus will be on films produced within (or evolving from) the Hollywood system. This will allow me to establish more meaningful links with the tradition of the musical genre as it has been traditionally understood. Pop music, as defined above, was an American British tradition which spread out all through the world, finding different accents in different places.

Moreover, sadly, for reasons of space it has also been necessary to exclude in the present project non-feature-length narratives such as the music video and, after considerable hesitation, also the serialized TV musical. This will help the volume's focus, leaving a fascinating area open for further study. Serialized TV narratives have become an important site in the past few decades to continue and question the musical's lineage, with hits like *Fame*, *Glee*, and *Empire*. These have raised important issues about genre, integration, and mythologies which are relevant to the discussions in this book, but they can't just be treated as if they worked in an identical way to feature films.

In order to answer some of the questions raised in this introduction, I will start by acknowledging the *difficulties* the Hollywood musical had in embracing the new kinds of music and then explore the effects of it finally embracing pop. In order to do that, I need to go back to the moment when it all started. Pop and the musical had an uneasy relationship for almost two decades, and this volume's chapter 1 focuses on the obstacles that hindered pop songs and the Hollywood musical from working together. Although film studios soon gestured tentatively towards the new rock singers (as early as 1955, Bill Haley's "Rock around the Clock" was heard over the credits of *The Blackboard Jungle* (1955), and Black rockers were showcased in the 1956 musical *The Girl Can't Help It*), pop was otherwise consigned to the margins of the studio system.

Early attempts at presenting pop music *within* the Hollywood musical are also examples of the failure to do so smoothly. So chapter 1 will turn around a certain perceived incompatibility in the 1960s between the demands of pop music and the demands of the musical as it was conceived by the Hollywood machinery. This chapter is about a struggle between the rising importance of pop music and the compromises it would take to make it a part of the Hollywood musical tradition, and Elvis will be a key exhibit to represent these tensions. To explore this idea, the chapter includes a brief consideration of the attitude implicit in the Broadway adaptation *Bye Bye Birdie*, released by Columbia in 1963. As in the original 1960s stage work, the film included a parody of Elvis, but in some ways there was a progression in Hollywood's attitude towards youth music. Elvis's career also evolved from the late 1950s to the early 1960s. The first sustained cycle of non-Elvis pop musicals somehow indebted to rock and roll comes with the AIP beach party series starring Frankie Avalon and Annette Funicello. Although successful on their own terms, they are further evidence that the worlds of pop music and the mainstream Hollywood musical were wide apart.

Chapter 2, "Embracing Pop," proposes three distinctive traditions within the pop musical that engage with music in different directions. First, pop styles are somehow assimilated into the *integrated* musical with interesting consequences: as we have seen in this introduction, the connotations brought in by pop music challenge some of the key tropes of traditional musicals. Secondly, *dance* is made central to narrative films. And, thirdly, the stabilization of a pop canon encourages a series of *biopics* on some of its key personalities. The integrated pop musical starts to deal with different themes and perspectives. I will refer to two different "integrated pop musicals" released decades apart, *The Rocky Horror Picture Show* and *Moulin Rouge!*, and assess the role of pop styles in the form. We shall notice how the attitude towards music and narrative changes in the intervening years. Dance had always figured centrally in the Hollywood musical, but putting all the weight of musical expression on dance only became a tradition in the pop musical after the success of *Saturday Night Fever*. This section deals briefly with two other contributions of dance to musicals: in the hip-hop–influenced *Beat Street* and the very mainstream *Dirty Dancing*. Finally, the trend for the musical biopic, which has been present in Hollywood since the late 1930s, becomes steeper as soon as pop discovers it has a past that can be anthologized. In a way, all three traditions contribute ways to "integrate" plot and music which are substantially different from the simple notion of integration that had been something of a doctrine, at least since the 1940s, in classical Hollywood. My key example here will be Dexter Fletcher's *Rocketman*, centering on Elton John, as it provides an excellent example of how popular songs are used to illuminate aspects of character and plot. The selections in this chapter aim for variety. Indeed, one of the starting points will be that the pop musical can only be sustained by using the different mythologies of pop music, so I have preferred to provide examples of films that use different aspects of pop: from glam rock, traditional rock, and hip-hop to disco and Latin pop.

After focusing on the difficult rise and on the achievements of the pop musical, chapter 3 will show instances in which the pop musical, like many established cycles, ends up being *about* pop music, pop stardom, and their legacies. Risking a truism, the pop musical's distinctiveness arises out of the distinctive experience of listening to pop music: its potential for engaging with politics, ethnic identities, and for confronting sexuality head-on. The three examples in this chapter explore different attitudes towards the past which endow the pop musical with specific energies. *Grease* appealed both to the 1978 youth market and those who had fond memories of the 1958 pop styles which the soundtrack referenced. By the late 1970s, earlier pop styles were associated with youth by the older generation. This trend then continued in subsequent years. My second and third examples are more interested in placing different pop styles within historical coordinates. In *Dreamgirls*, reviewing the Motown experience is used not just for nostalgia, but also to provide insights into the history of popular music, its deeply entrenched racism, and the conflict between the mainstream and personal expression. The last example will be *Velvet Goldmine*, another film that establishes a dialogue with pop music's history—in this case the demise of glam rock in 1974—and its power, by building its narrative on the reception of pop music and the way it can provide reference points for identity and pleasure, just as it aims for commercial success.

1   HOLLYWOOD AND THE RISE OF POP MUSIC

The Age of Elvis

The year 1954 was the year of the first mainstream broadcast hit by a white working-class youth from Tupelo, Mississippi, who had been earning a living as a truck driver, before signing up with Sam Phillips's Sun Records: a small label from Memphis specializing in country and African American music. The song, "That's All Right (Mama)," was originally written by Delta blues singer Arthur Crudup, and was then covered by Elvis Presley, who would go on to become rock's first megastar (and Hollywood's first pop crossover star). But in 1954, Presley was not considered a "rocker" as the term had not entered the mainstream: the singer was steeped in gospel, folk, blues, and hillbilly sounds he had heard since childhood, and he refused to underplay those influences. The often-told story of how he got his first career break makes it sound casual, as if it might as well not have happened at all, but it also marks one of the true watershed moments in American popular music. Elvis became a national obsession almost overnight, the focus of both positive and negative media attention, and he vividly represented the connotations of what was to be a new music. For (racist) white America, he sounded too Black; for concerned parents, his voice and his style hinted at the sexual knowledge they had so fiercely tried to conceal from their children, and there were those who even thought he was simply the devil incarnate.[1] But his fans were devoted. The newspapers tended to assume these were basically made up of screaming girls, but some elements of Elvis (coolness, machismo) were also fascinating to boys who wanted to *become* him.[2] The mystique he acquired after his irruption into American culture accompanied him until his last days.[3]

It was inevitable that Hollywood would see the potential for profit in the phenomenon, and Elvis himself thought the next logical step, after his breakout records, had to be the movies: the very concept of "rock star" had not even been introduced to popular culture yet, so stardom meant movies. However, film glory came at a price, and the results of Hollywood's interest in pop music during the next decade and a half were somewhat checkered. I will address the shortcomings and the opportunities these film texts represent as they attempt to use pop music and mythologies for musical storytelling.

Not unconnected to Elvis's debut the year before, 1955 has been widely regarded as a revolutionary year in popular music. However, this cannot just be explained away with one singer, no matter how legendary, recording a few songs, or even a handful of singers releasing a wave of innovative singles, no matter their success. In fact, many factors, cultural and social, were already in place, they just needed a catalyst to turn them into cultural debates, narratives, and imagery. Sounds, moods, or attitudes that had been there for years were made visible by shifts in the whole system. As noted in the introduction, these shifts also had to do with technology, makeovers in the industry structure, and the discovery of new audiences, resulting in a complete change in marketing strategies, the start of a new sound, and a new star system.[4] For thirty years the music business had been dominated by four large recording companies (RCA-Victor, Columbia, Capitol, and American Decca) but the exploration of new styles and the proliferation of local radio meant that from 1955 there was a surge of smaller companies showcasing the new sounds. These did not have, initially, the power of penetration the majors could wield. But at least they could make the big companies listen. New music men sought out and specialized in approaches to popular music that had been around but had not made it into the mainstream. The revolution in popular music in those years has now become the stuff of cultural mythologies and is featured in a number of self-referential pop musicals set in the years following 1955, including *Dreamgirls*, *Hairspray*, *The Buddy Holly Story*, *Great Balls of Fire!*, *Jersey Boys*, and *Walk the Line* (2005).

It's worth stating the obvious: the *lived* 1955 looked more like 1954 to contemporaries than it did to the mythical "1955" of twenty-first century studies. Elijah Wald's account usefully highlights this idea by providing numerous examples of overlap and confusion between the traditions of country, rhythm and blues, Tin Pan Alley standards, and rock and roll.[5] Original cast recordings from Broadway shows and film soundtracks remained big sellers for more than ten years after the rock revolution. The Marcels, a doo wop group, made a famous recording of Richard Rodgers and Lorenz Hart's "Blue Moon," and similarly The Platters, a vocal group often included in "early rock" anthologies, did some covers of old mainstream hits (including "Blue Moon" and "Smoke Gets in Your Eyes"). Clearly, the way different trends were labelled was fluid and did not coincide with current categories.

In Glenn C. Altschuler's view, rock and roll expressed too many aspects of experience that Hollywood had been reluctant to reflect, such as giving voice to the disempowered, challenging authority, and racism.[6] So early uses of rock and roll were cynical and used context to overlook the more sensitive issues rock brought to mind. Figureheads of the traditional media soon included rockers in their TV broadcasts. Elvis first appeared nationally on *The Stage Show* in January 1956, and, on April 3, 1956, on *The Milton Berle Show*. His performances on the legendary Ed Sullivan Show on September 9, 1956, on a programme watched by 82% of the audience, meant the final stamp of approval from the national media. Even if producers and cameramen struggled to keep Elvis's hips out of American homes, following complaints from angry spectators who rang up the broadcasting stations, he was at the center of the American popular media's imagination. Quickly, rock and roll was going mainstream and the power balance between the record industry and the film industry was starting to shift. Rock and roll made possible a parallel conception of popular music. In time the big companies started to produce and support this new "rock" music, but at the start it was all happening at smaller labels such as Sun Records and, from 1959, Motown.

The new voices and the new styles quickly made it into the movies. Bill Haley and the Comets' "Rock Around the Clock" was heard over the titles of *The Blackboard Jungle*, a film on "the youth problem," as early as 1955; Elvis was featured in his first film, *Love Me Tender*, in 1956 and would star in three subsequent films before being drafted into the army in

1958. A Columbia film using the Bill Haley hit song as its title and featuring Haley himself was released in 1956, directed by Fred F. Sears. *Rock Around the Clock* was about a manager's search for a "new sound" in the wake of the decadence of the old dance orchestras, with another slight plot featuring courting and jealousy attached. But what mattered were the musical numbers performed by Haley but also by The Platters, Freddy Bell, and Tony Martinez, as well as an appearance by Allan Freed, one of the key music men of the period and allegedly the originator of the expression "rock and roll." The late 1950s saw a cycle of other "jukebox" films in which rock and roll would be played (sometimes mixed with non-rock singers) and rock and roll music would soon become the preferred background music for youth films, particularly if juvenile delinquency was featured as it did in a handful of exploitation films.[7] Fox was the first large studio to explore this trend when they produced, in 1956, *The Girl Can't Help It*, directed by Frank Tashlin: half a comedy, starring Jayne Mansfield and Tom Ewell, and half a jukebox musical. In principle, the film is about the ridiculous rise of Mansfield's character to pop stardom (she simply screams shrilly into a microphone). This is, however, used as a framing story for the rock and roll performances. Still, when producing big budget musicals, Hollywood seemed to bet more heavily on Broadway fare, particularly pre-sold properties like the Rodgers and Hammerstein integrated musical plays, *West Side Story* and *The Music Man*, two 1957 Broadway shows transferred successfully to the screen with little changed for when they were released in 1961 and 1962 respectively.[8] There is, however, a particular example that demonstrates an attempt to introduce the new musical style within the traditional Broadway framework.

Bye Bye Birdie: *Broadway Looks Down on Pop*

The title sequence of the Columbia adaptation of *Bye Bye Birdie* is a good expression of old Hollywood's attitude to the rise of pop music. After Ann-Margret's solo lament, a montage of images of a hip-swiveling rock and roll performer, accompanied by buffo vocals, alternate with shots of Frank Sinatra frowning at the outrageousness of it all. Sinatra's dismissal of rock and roll had been harsh. He went on record in 1957 with the following verdict: "It's the most brutal, ugly, desperate, vicious form of expression it has been my misfortune to hear."[9] Sinatra would change his mind (and even invited Presley onto his TV show on the latter's return from army service), but his smug rejection would come to symbolize the antagonism between "old" and "new" popular music. For the teens represented in *Bye Bye Birdie*, Sinatra, who had been a teen idol himself, was now, irrevocably, old-fashioned, even uncool, a singer someone's parents would listen to (a later song, "Kids," set to a jaunty Charleston rhythm, also makes the generation gap comically explicit).

In the opening sequence of the film, whole armies of teenage girls demonstrate in front of the White House, screaming and protesting their idol Conrad Birdie's draft notice. This sequence was not included in the film's original stage source. The Broadway production made sense as a novelty entry in the 1960 season, but it was otherwise a very traditional show. It had a score by Charles Strouse, lyrics by Lee Adams, and libretto by Michael Stewart; it was directed by Gower Champion and starred Chita Rivera, Dick Van Dyke, Kay Medford, and Susan Watson, all Broadway pros unrelated to rock and roll music. Hollywood musicals had for a few years been favoring faithful transfers from Broadway. *Bye Bye Birdie* was the kind of slick integrated musical Broadway seemed to turn out every month throughout the 1950s: imbued with New York attitudes, sharp urban wit, and a slightly patronizing treatment of small-town America. It is in the city where the main characters (English teacher Albert Peterson and his girlfriend, secretary Rosie) see their future, and the display of adoration for the new pop music is focused on small-town America. If music styles had changed in radio and, by then, even on TV, with master influencer Ed Sullivan bringing rock and roll acts to his show, Broadway seemed unaware of the shift. Other important shows playing that season included *Camelot*, *The Unsinkable Molly Brown*, *Christine*, *Wildcat*, and *Tenderloin*. These were all set in the past: *Bye Bye Birdie* was an exception as it dealt with contemporary characters and situations. And even if rock and roll was then going through a slump commercially, it provided a good mythology for the times. Echoes of the new music could be heard in *Bye Bye Birdie's* instrumentation, which introduced guitars and other instruments to the sound which had not been frequent in traditional Broadway scoring.[10]

As in the case of the jukebox film musicals of previous years mentioned above, the project smacked of opportunism: the original project was a simple romantic comedy less marked by contemporary trends. But coming upon the idea of including references to Elvis was what made the project newly specific. The inspiration behind some aspects of the plot was actually Elvis's 1957 draft notice, issued at the peak of his popularity. In the stage show, an English teacher accidentally turned pop songwriter, supported by his lively Latino girlfriend of eight years, decides to write one last song for rock star Conrad Birdie before the latter goes off to the army.[11] The pop song, "One Last Kiss," is to be performed live at the Ed Sullivan Show, where the singer will kiss a teenager farewell before departing for army service, and hopefully, royalties will make everybody rich and allow the couple to finally marry. Pop is thus the background to a traditional musical plot of adults courting (there is a reluctance to commit that must be overcome). The selected teenager is sixteen-year-old Kim McAfee, from Sweet Apple, Ohio, a devoted fan of the singer. The show's subplot deals with the difficulties the stunt creates with Kim's boyfriend Hugo. The rest of the cast is made up of adults, including Albert's mother and Kim's parents.

Addressing the New York adult audience of the stage show, the rock and roll singer was portrayed in the play as vain, talentless, girl crazy, and dumb, little more than a PR stunt for gullible teens, with the adults constantly covering up his stupidity. Such characterization also affected the style of his songs: his simplistic tunes contrasted with the more sophisticated wordplay and the more elegant or uplifting melodies given to the leads. This presentation is supposed to elicit complicity from an adult mainstream audience, as well as the belief that they are in control of cultural trends: nobody should be worried about silly singers. We know now that there were changes afoot and a deep cultural shift had started, but audiences of the Broadway show were reassured by traditional sounds. For the show's adaptation to film in 1963, on the verge of the Beatles' revolution, some changes were introduced. Most importantly, even if the stars were still played by established performers (Dick Van Dyke from the Broadway show and Hollywood actress Janet Leigh[12]), the marketing campaign was based on up-and-coming Ann-Margret.

The film's version of Kim is undeniably sexy in contrast with the sweet, more naïve Susan Watson who played the role on Broadway. Ann-Margret had already made a name on the "rock" scene and had been billed as "the female Elvis;" she had a recording of "Jailhouse Rock" to her name. A few years before her film debut, she had recorded with The Jordanaires, who had been Elvis's backup group. She then went on to play parts in two films: the sentimental *A Pocketful of Miracles* (1961) and the Rodgers and Hammerstein musical *State Fair* (1962), the latter a remake of their 1945 film musical in which she played the "modern" showgirl and had her songs jazzed up. Ann-Margret signals a change in spirit to the original in order to accommodate the new "pop." For the *Bye Bye Birdie* film, she was given a new title song (figure 1.1), oddly placed outside of the narrative as a kind of prologue performed before a blue screen and repeated in a short epilogue; her image became iconic. In her book on rock on the Broadway stage, Elizabeth L. Wollman insists there is balance between the adults and the kids of the original.[13] For the Hollywood version, teenagers are more prominent; besides Ann-Margret, the film also cast popular pop singer Bobby Rydell as Hugo. Producers altered the New York balance of the original to achieve broader appeal, particularly in the heartlands. It was Ann-Margret, not the first-billed adult stars, who dominated the film poster and the film soundtrack LP, who was subsequently featured on the cover of *Life* magazine, and who became one of the most talked-about stars of that year. After *Bye Bye Birdie*, she would go on to star in *Viva Las Vegas* (1964) alongside Presley (figure 1.2), and, much later, carried her pop persona into the film adaptation of the rock opera *Tommy*. Ann-Margret is thus a good illustration of the tension between Hollywood and pop that is central to this chapter: on the one hand she carried some of the connotations of pop, but on the other she could not manage to sustain a full career in the movies based on those credentials. Still, the casting of Ann-Margret in *Bye Bye Birdie* contributes to a change in the play's

Fig. 1.1: A star is born. Ann-Margret in *Bye Bye Birdie*.

Fig. 1.2: Male and female Elvises. *Viva Las Vegas!*

original connotations: teenagers displace adults as the focus of the film, and despite her engaging performance, there are hints that this Kim might not be as naïve as the script may lead us to think.

Bye Bye Birdie did not dismiss a teen audience outright, as the adult-targeted Broadway show had done. Although at the start they appear as a screaming crowd, the first number in Sweet Apple is the fun "The Telephone Hour." Written and scored in the spunky idiom of girl-group singing, the number links together a group of teenagers who gossip about Kim and Hugo "going steady."[14] Of course, they appear as immature, even silly, kids, but there is a charm here which sharply contrasts with the sterner dismissals of teen music in the press. As if driven by the new attitudes, even the mise en scène seems to adopt certain stylistic traits of 1960s pop aesthetics: Brady Bunch–style grids, flat compositions, primary colours, and even some animated moments (figures 1.3, 1.4). The teenagers had a voice in the original, here their voice is made even more distinctive. Janet Leigh and Dick Van Dyke, as the young courting couple, are still carrying the action, but the kids carry the film. Even if they are caricatures, simplistic and overdone, the tone of the film also makes the adults (including the kids' parents and the town's mayor) look ridiculous. Musicals add dimensions to characters through the skill and energy performers display in their musical numbers. If "The Telephone Hour" was cute, a later number with the teens, "A Lot of Livin' to Do," provides Ann-Margret with an opportunity to show off her jazzy dancing persona and it injects the kind of life into the plot that the adults can't compete with. Conrad,

Fig. 1.3: "Pop-ing it up." *Bye Bye Birdie.*

Fig. 1.4: Pop graphics in *Bye Bye Birdie.*

the "Elvis" character, is also featured in this number. For a few minutes, we see the possibilities of the rock and roll persona. The song, cool and driven by percussion, is about liberation from the adults, and for once in the film there doesn't seem to be any doubts about the urgency of such a liberation. Rock and roll in this film is no mere object of ridicule: it has *meaning*.

Still, if the film is more empathetic with the teens than the stage show, no love is reserved for the Elvis figure. The rock singer Conrad Birdie (played by Jesse Pearson) is still portrayed as mostly devoid of charm and his numbers, especially "Honestly Sincere," are even shriller than they'd been onstage. The song, shot to suggest the excesses of a religious revival, is, ironically, about the singer's insincerity. Given rock's later emphasis on authenticity, the choice of a theme for the singer's main song is telling. "Honestly Sincere" proffers "authenticity" (long before it became central to rock's mythologies), to dismiss it through performance and characterization. The character's phoniness is obvious also in the plot, so "sincerity," we are told, is just a pose for rock singers. The parody of Elvis is cartoonish, and it consistently fails to account for the fascination the original elicited. Instead, it focuses on his crassness and lack of wit, making audiences who gasp and faint at each hip-swiveling motion seem even sillier. And it is not irrelevant that at the film's closure, Kim returns to her more homely boyfriend and Conrad is packed up to the army while the adults can get on with their lives. In the world of Bye Bye Birdie, rock and roll is a phase to be overcome. After the "happily ever after" number for the adults, Kim/Ann-Margret returns to us in front of the blue screen to sing the title song with revised lyrics: these now claim that she is also moving on. She will remain a sexy modern woman, but she is cured from her fascination with rock singers and will devote her love to, as another song goes, "One Boy."

But Bye Bye Birdie is also an important integrated musical in that it embraces the new styles (rock and roll and doo wop) as tools for characterization. Thereafter, pop becomes the language of contemporary youths and the Tin Pan Alley style will only be intuitively used for the past: in The Sound of Music (1965) teenagers sing showtunes, but this is justified by its wartime setting. The same logic applies to Oliver! (1968). From 1968, the very idea of traditional showtunes being sung by contemporary young characters starts to become unacceptable. Bye Bye Birdie, even when it looks down on pop, acknowledges it is the new youth language and powerfully uses lexicon taken from musical theatre. Recent stage shows like Hamilton demonstrate that pop styles constitute a repertoire that can broaden the possibilities for characterization. Bye Bye Birdie is the first example of a Broadway show acknowledging a need for pop music and its ability to represent contemporary situations.[15]

Clearly, American show business could only see rock and roll, at best, as just another form of show business, to be understood on the terms dictated by mainstream ideologies. The film remains a one-off, the only attempt to find a, somewhat brittle, compromise between pop music and the Broadway style for a decade. Rock and roll was accepted as a form of razzle dazzle, but within this context, it lacked any kind of progressive impulse. Inevitably, if somewhat reluctantly, the film seems to have taken on the sounds, energy, and newness of the teen rebellion. Just as *Bye Bye Birdie* was experiencing a transformation from mainstream Broadway to mainstream Hollywood, Elvis, the real one, was also transitioning.

Elvis: From Rock Icon to Hollywood Star

As noted above, Elvis's persona was loaded with layers of meaning: working class, Southern, rural, rebel, sexy, seductive, talented, successful. Not all of these connotations fitted well with the preferred personae of Hollywood stars, although some critics saw in him qualities that recalled a singing version of James Dean or Marlon Brando. The press could not stop talking about his hips, his voice, his hair, his youth, his smirk, his roughness, and all of this was interpreted in terms of impending social change.[16] He was very different from other pop singers aimed at the teen demographic, like the equally popular, "immaculately" white Pat Boone. Elvis was not the only one to convey this new set of meanings. Other names, some of them with substantial careers behind them by 1955, would join the revolution: Bill Haley, Little Richard, Buddy Holly, and Jerry Lee Lewis, for instance. Still, Elvis would be the one with the mythical aura when the first wave of the rock and roll revolution was underway.[17] Elvis ruled the airwaves for a few years, then the army called, causing distress to a generation of teens.

By 1962 it was easy, or at least possible, for adult mainstream audiences to believe rock and roll had been a passing phase. Traditional Broadway adaptations seemed in favour again: *West Side Story* was a big hit in 1961 and a version of *My Fair Lady* (1964) was in the works. On the other hand, the payola scandals[18] left small labels in a difficult position and big companies started to offer alternatives.[19] It had been nine years since Elvis broke out onto the scene, the image parodied by "Conrad Birdie" had been long left behind. His newer films, like *G.I. Blues* (1960), *Blue Hawaii* (1961), and *Roustabout* (1964), while wildly successful, presented a blander, candy-colored version of the singer pouting around a range of exotic surroundings and tourist attractions.[20] Even his musical repertoire was changing. His other 1964 offering, *Viva Las Vegas*, co-starring Ann-Margret, was produced by MGM and directed by Freed Unit veteran George Sidney. What happened here was that mainstream musicals had at first attempted to use the "authentic" Elvis mythologies, but a change of heart seemed to have taken place as the 1950s ended. The gap between "rock and roll Elvis" and "film star Elvis" would further illustrate the difficulties of the Hollywood establishment to embrace pop-based musicals.

Elvis's Hollywood career is thus naturally divided into two distinct, unequal periods, separated by his two-year stint in the army. The four films he made before going into the army in 1958 somehow attempt to capitalize on his original rocker image, providing him with roles that take up different aspects of the singer's legend. In *Love Me Tender*, his first film, he plays a supporting role (the main character's brother), but the film uses his "country" image as one way to establish the film's western genre with songs. The three most important films in consolidating his star image followed. *Loving You* (1957), *Jailhouse Rock* (1957), and *King Creole* (1958) are exceptional for their engagement with the singer's working-class roots and the threat he posed to white middle-class America, as few musicals had done before. For the second period, after his return from army service in 1960, he made acting the focus of his career, and until his 1969 "comeback" performances, he would make about three films every year.

Although his first three films as a star have intrinsic interest and tend to present different sides of the Elvis legend, I will focus primarily on *Jailhouse Rock*. Just as the other two, it deals with the working-class protagonist's rise to stardom. The film reads as the fullest blow-by-blow account, the one that comes closest to the image created around the singer: each of the elements that would go on to feature in publicity campaigns are here, and in turn the film acts as a publicity stunt in consolidating that image. We first see protagonist Vince Everett driving a truck, in a rather literal reference to Presley's pre-Sun Records métier. Links between off-screen persona and onscreen character were common in his early films, but seldom so blatant. All in all, Elvis plays the same character throughout his career, even if the contexts vary greatly from Seattle (in 1963's *It Happened at the World Fair*) to some exotic country in the Middle East in *Harum Scarum* (1965). Although not an inventive or complex actor, even in his early films he has an intriguing screen presence. Snapshots from other films are also pieces in a puzzle that represents the Elvis myth: In

King Creole, his character leaves school before completing his studies and his father is unable to provide for the family; in *Loving You* it is the reaction of female audiences that propels the young singer to the top. The three films unapologetically present the singer's southern roots, although *King Creole* places him in the city of New Orleans, whereas the others feature the star as a small-town boy. In all three, a link between country music and other southern traditions is clearly in place, although Black music is only featured in *King Creole*.[21]

Although the attempt to turn the singer into a film star is clear, what distinguishes these films are their emphasis on the "bad boy" image that Dean and Brando were also promoting in those years. *Jailhouse Rock*'s inciting incident is an outburst of violence where Vince is provoked into a fistfight (in defense of a woman's honour) that will earn him a jail sentence. David L. James has remarked on the continuous fistfights the Elvis character gets into, almost a recurring motif in the Elvis filmography.[22] Indeed, violence was one of the effects of the new music most often discussed in the conservative press, although it seems to have been part of a fantasy rather than something real. Imagining the rocker as somebody who could inflict violence on average citizens was tempting. Violence in the early Elvis films was acknowledged by producers to be something that would give his characters some edge, and in turn it contributed to his star persona, along the lines of other 1950s "rebels" such as Dean or Brando. Elvis comes across initially as a mild-mannered, gentle, southern boy. The fistfights are there to endow his character with strength and traditional masculine traits. The outbursts are an attempt to "have it both ways," in typical Hollywood fashion: depending on the audience Elvis could be seen as either a threat or an icon. By introducing these traits, Hollywood helped craft an image for Elvis that became particularly disruptive within the genre, which usually preferred more elegant, ambitious, or articulate leading men.

Vince spends some time in jail, and there he strikes up a rapport with old-timer country singer Hunk Houghton (Mickey Shaughnessy). Hunk is characterized as knowledgeable yet rough and becomes something of a mentor for the young kid. Hunk is also dishonest and jealous of the newcomer, and Vince will pay him back for that when he comes out of jail: this makes for some bitterness, even for some discomfort amongst unprepared audiences. The climax of the film comes when a disgruntled Houghton strikes Vince, damaging his throat and rendering him unable to sing. The way the friendship ends up in conflict can be read as a comment on Elvis's individuality: even if his roots were in old hillbilly traditions represented by Houghton, he soon developed them into something more personal. The character learns his art from the old country singer and somehow builds up a career based on the older man's teachings. His rise to fame, however, happens only when he finds his own kind of music, as illustrated by a scene in the recording studio that parallels elements of the Elvis legend: he attempts a song, which does not work, as he is too aware of the technology and the pressure around him, but as soon as he can improvise and "be himself," the recording is a success.

When he becomes famous, his first television appearance shows him performing "Jailhouse Rock," surrounded by spirited, artificial choreography courtesy of Jack Cole, a Broadway legend who had worked in several musical sequences with Marilyn Monroe. The mood is comic, an attempt to offset the song's rougher, more dangerous elements. Moments like this show a certain hesitation about the Elvis persona. This was one of Elvis's legend-making songs and therefore a popular title that would ensure box office returns. That the film chose "Jailhouse Rock" as its title and key number to show Vince's triumph, is a sign of the tension between the need to "use" the legend and the pressures to make Elvis conform to the more light-hearted impulses of the mid-fifties' musical. While not an integrated number, it does point to the star's central mytheme of dangerous origins and edgy influences while also reassuring conservative audiences.

All three films have strong older women assisting the Elvis character's success, although they are complemented with younger, meeker, more innocent love interests. In *Loving You* and *Jailhouse Rock*, these women are both talent scouts. They have mixed motivations to push the young singer into stardom. Experienced music woman Lizabeth Scott in *Loving You* "discovers" the young, raw performer and will develop a rapport with him, but ultimately her heart belongs to her ex-husband (Wendell Corey), the singer she was representing before engaging Elvis. Elvis's love interest is represented by the younger, less "professional" Susan, a backup singer played by Dolores Hart. In *Jailhouse Rock* a similar situation develops. The talent scout here (Peggy) is played by Judy Tyler, and she also has ambivalent designs. Peggy appears as an opportunist and her motivations are so slippery that at one point the singer dismisses her, so in the later part of the film Vince is seen keeping both of his mentors at a distance. As it was the case with the singer's image, these films seem to want to have it both ways. On the one hand, the strong women need to be somewhat in love with the young singer, even when they are not being completely honest; on the other hand, Elvis needs a traditional girlfriend who won't boss him around. The result is that the singer's independence and individuality triumphs over his influences.[23] More than in *Loving You*, *Jailhouse Rock* develops the love interest plot line in an ambivalent way. For long sections, Peggy is seen as someone who does not quite support Vince and even compromises his art. Although she supports him in his breakout recording, it is only by putting her aside for a while that Vince can reach stardom.

Although it would be excessive to label them integrated musicals, these films make good narrative use of rock and roll and pop ballads: they would not make sense with a less contemporary score and certainly Elvis sings the kinds of songs he had become associated with. Sometimes the films try to go beyond the showcase format, and they gesture towards tighter integration. But more importantly, they are less about communicating a specific story as they are about the Elvis legend and his style. Anything that Elvis sings, no matter its origin, somehow becomes "Elvis-ized;" the working-class protagonists are always on the verge of delinquency, and jail is present in all three films. *King Creole* might be the more daring one in presenting his dealings with underground gangster bosses (figure 1.5) and for the melodramatic moment in which the older woman dies in his arms.

The second period of Elvis's career consisted of 27 films made between 1960 and 1969, with repetitive plot motives and characterizations. It is hard to make great claims for their quality or originality, and after *Viva Las Vegas*, they become increasingly lazy, the casts less interesting, the musical selections less characteristic of Elvis. Watching some of the later ones, like *Harum Scarum*, or *Charro!* (1969), makes non-devotees suspect nobody believed in the project or was putting in any effort. In *Charro!*, for instance, Elvis only sings the title song; and the plot of *Harum Scarum*, set in a Middle Eastern country and involving a coup d'etat reminiscent of Alexander Korda's *The Thief of Bagdad* (1940), is ridiculous even by Elvis's standards. Still, taken as a group, they are interesting as symptoms of the disconnect in the relationship between rock

Fig. 1.5: Noir Elvis. *King Creole.*

and roll and the musicals of the period: clearly Hollywood was trying to approach a different demographic and though it acknowledged that this required changes, it was uncertain about how to implement them. Not only are we dealing with a different kind of male star, the whole relationship between the musical numbers and the plot seems to have moved away from the standards of the Freed Unit.

For years, Elvis's Hollywood films have been harshly dismissed by critics. Even one of the staunchest Elvis defenders, Greil Marcus, sees the movies as something of an embarrassment.[24] Indeed, the films are so loose and star-centric that they do not fit with any strict notion of the musical as a genre from Altman's specific syntactic or semantic elements. But even these opinions suggest that Elvis had a very special place in the development of the pop musical: many musicals after the early 1970s have shown a similar disregard for conventions. In the sixties, Elvis was the exception: the moment the musical consolidated its pop credentials around a star. Let us remember that these are the years of hits such as *Bye Bye Birdie*, *Mary Poppins* (1964), *My Fair Lady*, *The Sound of Music*, *Funny Girl* (1968), and *Oliver!*. Most of these films' stars came from the Broadway or London stage: Dick Van Dyke, Julie Andrews, Rex Harrison, Barbra Streisand, Shani Wallis. Elvis was a rare case: a pop singer who starred consistently in mainstream Hollywood musicals without a Broadway pedigree. David L. James analyzes exhaustively the narrative motifs from this section of Elvis's career, describing the systematic motives and how these were both kept alive and used to re-shape the singer's image.[25] Violence is a recurring pattern, but as James reminds us, the characters now only fight "if they have to." The elements of threat associated with the early Elvis are largely inexistent now: we have the rougher characters in the early *Roustabout*, and memories of his country image recur in *Flaming Star* (1960) and in the late *Charro!*, but the more typical image is represented in *Blue Hawaii*, where he plays the son of a pineapple plantation owner who becomes a tour guide as an act of rebellion.[26]

His relationships with women have also changed in this second phase. Gone are the cougars and ambivalent talent scouts of *Loving You* and *Jailhouse Rock*, and so too the conflicted, ambivalent feelings, now replaced by a long line of younger, prettier starlets including Jo Ann Mobley, Jill St. John, and Stella Stevens. When an older woman appears to be interested in Elvis, as in *Blue Hawaii*, it turns out to be a false impression: she actually has feelings for someone her own age. In most films there are a number of girls chasing Elvis, thus somehow keeping alive the legend of his independence, although eventually he settles for one, often the homelier one. In *It Happened at the World Fair*, he needs to polish his uncouth ways to gain the affection of a nurse. And in *Change of Habit*, he plays a doctor so saintly that his partner has to be Mary Tyler Moore playing a nun. In all of these there is a process of taming the star, replacing his energy and sex appeal for the clichés of married love. These films even flirt with old Hollywood stardom with supporting parts given to the likes of Angela Lansbury (*Blue Hawaii*) and Barbara Stanwyck (*Roustabout*). His sensual movements become less and less central to the characters he plays. He is sometimes partnered with children. Whereas the early Elvis hinted toward dangerous aspects of class and sexuality, these later films just use the Elvis image as a powerful magnet which carries more conventional meanings: by the time of *Charro!* and *Change of Habit*, any connotations of authenticity had gone. Though authenticity had been central to the Elvis myth, this did not prevent the films' soundtracks from becoming best sellers or cause his popularity to decrease. Elvis retained a mystique, even if the situations and characterizations are far from what we associate with the original Elvis. Even after he had left behind his revolutionary edge, his blander persona was being embraced by some devoted fans.

What we find in the transition from his early to his later career, is the force of some elements of the Hollywood musical taking hold of the Elvis persona. And this needs to be said: the success of the films perversely proved that one did not need to be a rocker or a good actor in order to be embraced by an audience. The story of Elvis is similar to many show-business stories, including those of Al Jolson, Ethel Merman, Judy Garland, and Madonna: personalities so strong that audiences just can't get enough of them despite their limitations. No matter what their public images, their connotations, or aesthetics, they demand to be seen and enjoyed. On the other hand, his films are a good illustration of the hesitations of the Hollywood industry when faced with the challenge of doing something with rock and roll. But if the Hollywood mainstream could not cope with the rise of pop, maybe smaller companies could. The alternative to Elvis was to be found in a series of films made outside the Hollywood studios, somewhere with less baggage.

The Youth Musical: The AIP "Beach Party" Cycle

The merging of the worlds of pop and the musical needs to be understood within the wider context of the rise of the teenager in American culture: first as a relatively problematic type, later as a devoted consumer. Although primarily aimed at the youth market, Elvis's films were not what was increasingly understood as "youth" films. Of course, teenagers had been featured in films before, but by the mid-fifties, as we shall see, "the teenager" was, in Foucaultian parlance, *a new species* at the center of a dense discursive network. The new teenagers, as discussed in the press and by scientific experts, were both a site for cultural anxieties and, especially, a new market which would quickly be addressed by Hollywood. After a brief flourish in the mid-1950s, with *Rebel Without a Cause* (1955) and the early rock and roll films as major exhibits, the youth market was abandoned by the major studios who were intent on addressing broader audiences (this was mostly manifested in terms of exploitation movies). The new demographics revealed by the rise of rock and roll was addressed, from that point onwards, by smaller upstart companies. American International Pictures (AIP) was the most successful of them. Created in 1954 and founded by Samuel Z. Arkoff and James H. Nicholson, it catered to younger audiences with cheaply produced genre films in which the protagonists

were normally teenagers. Normally these would explore areas less fre-
quented by mainstream Hollywood films: juvenile delinquency, horror, some
cheap westerns, science fiction, adding to these a change in perspective.
Rather than having obedient kids under the authority of adults, young
characters tended to be the heroes, points of identification for equally
young audiences. By 1960, the company was well established, and they
even attempted some "quality" horror films, mostly starring Vincent Price,
using the works of Edgar Allan Poe as a prestige factor. This was followed,
from 1963, by a series of youth musicals, frequently directed by William
Asher, which became extremely popular. Although dismissed by many
historians, they provide another diagnostic of the tensions between pop
and the Hollywood musical at the time: they follow up on traditions within
the Hollywood musical and they were very influential in future developments of the genre.[27]

As noted, youth musicals were nothing new. Starting in the late 1930s,
and inspired by even earlier Broadway trends, sub-genres were cultivated
by major studios which included *Too Many Girls* (1940), *Girl Crazy* (1943),
Babes in Arms (1939), and *Good News* (1947). Typically, these were about
groups of kids (two of those titles star Mickey Rooney and Judy Garland)
who got together and pooled their resources for a cause. In order to
achieve their aims they often needed to put on a show. For instance, in
Babes on Broadway (1941), Rooney has to decide between socially
responsible work with the community or becoming a Broadway star. In
typical Hollywood fashion (and in perfect illustration of the genre's ideological underpinning, as identified by Feuer) he achieves both, but in the
course of the plot he has to make grown-up decisions. This was before
the idea of the teenager had acquired its mid-1950s connotations, and
the character arcs in these films are about becoming more responsible
and mature. Youth is just the seed for the future, a stage one must get
through before one becomes a "proper" (i.e., adult) person. The conflict
between the energy of youth and the responsibilities of adult life is particularly obvious in the Mickey and Judy musicals. Both their treatment of
character arcs and their engagement with a particular idea of youth mark
a difference between the classic youth musicals and the AIP "beach
party" cycle. Kids here have no particular drive to achieve anything; they
are uncommitted to any cause, and the musicals don't work too hard at
considering labor relationships.

The beach party cycle seems to take place in a youth utopia where there exist a few adults (who are often ridiculous or mean) but no parents. Good-looking young people cavort on sandy beaches, sunbathe, surf, and get sentimentally (but never too deeply) attached. As Gary Morris proposes, the beach location brings with it an important set of connotations:

The films thus exist far from the headlines of the day, in a never-never land of white leisure-class youth, reaping the postwar profits of their parents' hard work and studious conformity to enjoy the pure sensations of innocent irresponsibility (however brief) and sanitized romance.[28]

We are dealing here with a very specific "mythical kingdom," that places the cycle theoretically within the fairy tale variety, rather than grouping it with the Mickey and Judy folk musicals. This kind of setting was already present, albeit sonically, in the early 1960s "surf music" genre, one of the many varieties developed during the rock and roll slump at the end of the 1950s. Surf music was mindless and trivial, but it powerfully engaged with an idealized way of life which participated in certain Pacific Islands traditions (surf culture was born in Hawaii, then imported to the West Coast). The moods and lyrics of this type of music helped the listener to imagine a certain image of the Californian beaches (contrasting with previous versions of the same location in film noir[29]), which is one of the key mythemes of the 1960s in America: California was sunny, liberal, relaxed. The vision was already present in a series of "surf" films set in Hawaii or California, such as *Gidget* (1959) or *Ride the Wild Surf* (1964), and would become a staple of American film into the 1970s and beyond. Musically, in the early 1960s, the key representatives of surf music and/or the California myth were The Beach Boys, and although their film career was limited to some guest spots (the group's leader Brian Wilson has a non-singing cameo in the AIP's *How to Stuff a Wild Bikini*), their influence on the beach party cycle is palpable.

The series stars Frankie Avalon and Annette Funicello (figure 1.6). Avalon was discovered as a "rock" singer in 1958 by Bob Marcucci, one of the early rock and roll music men, who specialized in the mellower side of the spectrum. Avalon, twenty-three at the time, had already had two number one hits at the time of *Beach Party* (1963) and had been in some

Fig. 1.6: Frankie Avalon and Annette Funicello in *Beach Blanket Bingo*.

high-profile films like *El Alamo* (1960). Funicello was under contract with Disney. She was a regular in the Mickey Mouse Club, and her loan to AIP was made under very restrictive terms: not just for her character's sense of sexual propriety and what she was supposed to wear, but even for specifying the language to be used around her during the shoot. The rest of the cast is made up of youthful types, like Jody McRea, who plays a character known as Bonehead: naïve and dim-witted, the butt of every joke. Adult performers were borrowed from more mainstream avenues. As in the Elvis cycle, established performers such as Paul Lynde, Buddy Hackett, Martha Hyer, Dorothy Malone, Vincent Price, Peter Lorre, Keenan Wynn, Mickey Rooney, and Buster Keaton all have appearances in the series, sometimes in mere cameos, broadening the films' appeal. And then there are the antagonists. Although mostly different for each film, the leather-clad biker gang led by Eric Von Zipper (Harvey Lembeck) are a recurring group. The inspiration for them was Brando's character in *The Wild One* (1953), and in the film the whole gang, but particularly the leader, appear as pompous, vain, terminally stupid bullies who are out-witted by the kids at every turn. This indicates, on the one hand, a typical AIP intention to make the kids the film's main point of entry, but also a faint attempt to place the films within more adult marketing structures.

The storylines in the cycle are not exactly similar, but they are simi-larly predictable and their avowed looseness (in his overview of the cycle, Gary Morris calls them "anarchic"[30]) mean they can be seen in terms of pieces that recur throughout several films. The kids seem to be living in an endless summer, in a rented beach house with no parental interference. Plot complications are slight. In *Muscle Beach Party* (1964), the kids have to compete with a muscle boy gym next door; in the latter as in *Beach Party*, *Beach Blanket Bingo* (1965), and *Bikini Beach* (1964), they are watched by adults who want to "study them." This is interesting, as that section of the plot tends to backfire on these grown-up observers, who are consistently won over. The adult gaze turns out to be less authoritative than it thinks it is. In *Beach Party*, it is Robert Cummings's anthropologist who uses high tech to write a study of the group which, when summarized by his assistant, seems to be largely about teen sex. In *Beach Blanket Bingo*, Paul Lynde plays an agent who wants to make use of the kids' talents, whereas in *Bikini Beach,* a conservative newspaper editor (Keenan Wynn) wants to prove that the kids are no more intelligent than his chimpanzee. All of these attempts are revealed as mistaken or ridiculous and the kids always get the upper hand: these are perfect examples of genre films that clearly know their audience.[31]

Besides the beach, there are at least two other important locations which reappear across the series. The main one is a café, which is where most of the musical numbers take place. In a provocative article on the ideology of the cycle, R. L. Rutsky identifies traits of the cafés that bring to mind "beat" cafés and Greenwich Village dives, thus associating the kids with counterculture rather than the system.[32] Another location that features throughout the series is the shack where the bikers, led by Eric Van Zipper, meet at the billiard table. The billiard table, used as the paradigm of coolness in films by Brando and Paul Newman, is here used for comic purposes. Besides the conflicts with the adults, there are constant clashes with the bikers, and the films tend to conclude with a chase scene.

At least occasionally the films dare to showcase Black musicians, which makes them more ethnically diverse than late Elvis films and a sign of the advantages of working outside the big studios. A very young Stevie Wonder is featured in *Bikini Beach* and *Muscle Beach Party*. The rest of the singing is taken up by Avalon and Funicello (each have at least one solo and there's a duet for each film) and some guest singers like Donna Loren. Loren was basically a recording artist and only appears in the films to sing one or two generic songs, as do a series of guest groups including Dick Dale and his Del Tones and The Kingsmen, which link the film to the earlier jukebox cycle. The songs are seldom integrated,[33] and the choreography is both energetic and simple rather than elegant or sophisticated. Some numbers may have a certain structure, as in the title sequence for *Beach Blanket Bingo*, but otherwise the way the films portray teen dancing is far from the spectacular, thought-through choreographies of older musicals. This "dirty" style will be used for musical numbers in pop musicals with increasing frequency. Numbers are closer to a "slice of life" and sometimes it is easy to see a structure or a center, as if the camera is looking for a position as unartistic as possible. Prime examples of this are the title number for *Fame*, the hip-hop numbers of *Beat Street*, or the "Magic Night" number in *Can't Stop the Music*. One of the influences of pop in the musical, although not every time, is precisely to blur the difference between choreography and rhythm, as well as the boundary between musical numbers and storyline.

The AIP beach party cycle is thus a point of convergence between youth films, pop music, and the beach mythologies, which reinforce each other, creating new ways to reach an audience. In spite of their lack of artistic ambition, they are still fondly remembered, and they are key references in later films, including *Grease*, which uses some of the films' narrative motives (and features a Frankie Avalon cameo), the spoof *Psycho Beach Party* (2000), and the Disney-produced diptych *Teen Beach Movie*, in which two surfing kids are teleported to what looks like an AIP beach party musical. *Teen Beach Movie* has some fun with the cycle, as its simplistic cavorting is lightly mocked and occasionally experienced as a nightmare.

In an early characterization of the beach party films, Gary Morris concludes that the whole cycle is just a fantasy of stability for convoluted times: loose and undisciplined, but reinforcing reactionary ideas about sex and society.[34] Rather than fully engaging with the rock and roll ethos, the films were something of an antidote to what was perceived as a dangerous culture. Although some of his points are well argued, they need to be complemented by R. L. Rutsky's argument in a 1999 article, which identifies new possibilities:

> Indeed, in these films, the appeal of surfing and surf subculture is often based on the attractiveness of nonconformist, irreverent and anti-bourgeois attitudes cobbled together from elements of

teenage culture, rock and roll, bohemian philosophy, and beat culture, mixed with a heavy dose of parody. This appeal is, moreover, linked to the allure of non-Western cultures, derived in large part from surfing's own Pacific Island origins.[35]

With these insights we are getting closer to another of the central ideas in the characterization of the musical as a genre: its creation of a utopia. And even if the literal meanings conveyed by a plot are conservative, we could argue, the musical counters them with a more general invitation to campy, self-aware, sexy fun, with music a part of that life. Escapism it is, but as Richard Dyer reminds us, escapism can have its uses, and despite their silly plots (or maybe *because* of them), these films open up a world of possibilities. One of the developments of the genre consisted of shattering this idea of utopia which seemed so central to the fairy tale musical. It's as if the arcadia had turned into a dangerous forest where things can go wrong: in many pop musicals, hints of utopia are revealed as flawed or fake.[36]

Elvis Presley, Conrad Birdie, Ann-Margret, Frankie Avalon, and the AIP youth musicals are all symptoms of the particular set of circumstances in the 1960s, whereby pop music and the Hollywood musical seemed to inhabit different realities and where attempts to bridge them were neither committed nor successful. Taken individually, they also suggest reasons for the failure to integrate pop music and film, one of the issues that musicals, whatever their style, have always had to contend with. Elvis needed to be *de-Elvisized*; Ann-Margret became just another musical diva with some cooler edge; Conrad Birdie was not even a serious attempt at parody; Frankie Avalon softened any trace of rock and roll, for an image that was even blander than Elvis's at his blandest; and the AIP musicals all existed in a bubble, turning their backs to conventional movies, real situations, and real people.

These are the reasons for the lack of a substantial use of pop music in the Hollywood musical. But there were also suggestions that pointed towards a future for pop music: *Bye Bye Birdie* suggested that there were uses for pop music in characterization and storytelling; Elvis, even in his less interesting films, highlighted the fascination of the rock singer as a star, by bringing interesting connotations to that role; and even the AIP musicals, which were chaotically plotted and had less interesting stars, introduced a particular kind of musical utopianism that, soon, would be hard to convey through other kinds of music. And when one takes all of these elements together, one film immediately comes to mind: *Grease*. It is perhaps the sum, the eventually successful result, of these previously failed explorations in search of new relationships between pop music and the Hollywood industry. But between the beach party cycle and its most successful descendant, other changes affecting pop music, film, and politics emerged around 1968, and they were represented by a Broadway show that harnessed the energies of rock to the musical.

2   EMBRACING POP

Integrating the Pop Musical

Pop Comes of Age

Traditionally, the Hollywood musical had always borrowed from Broadway for innovation, for prestige, and to obtain new personalities. In 1968 the Broadway musical finally embraced pop: *Hair*—a rock revue riffing on themes from the counterculture—transferred from Joe Papp's public theatre to the Great White Way, and the relationship between rock and "the musical" changed forever. And, unlike the bland AIP musicals of recent years, this show featured key elements of the updated rock ethos, thus opening the floodgates for countercultural attitudes in mainstream entertainment.[1]

Hair was a sure sign that the Von Trapps and the Dickensian orphans, the big ladies with a mission and a hat, and the superannuated stage divas no longer spoke or sung the language of the times: they were not just uncool, but downright reactionary. This new "tribal rock" musical was about everything the Broadway musical and its Hollywood counterpart had been repressing for over ten years: earnestness, social awareness, politics, race, sex, rock, and drugs. Devised by two hippy actors, James Rado and Gerome Ragni, for the off-Broadway circuit, it was musicalized by Galt MacDermot, who was close to the conventions of musical theatre.[2] *Hair* was a huge success, but the assimilation of pop music conventions into the sustained spectacle and dramatic structure of the stage musical was not instant. To start with, the play's dramatic arc is unapologetically thin, which seemed to go along with the widespread notion that rock was not good for storytelling: rock, it was assumed, was about an attitude, not a story.

This chapter explores three modes within the Hollywood pop musical, all of which became consistent trends in the seventies. All engage with ways to make pop music a part of a film narrative. Two of them—the integrated pop musical and the pop musical biopic—were part of the Hollywood tradition, although the pop era brought significant changes to their conception and structure. I will pay particular attention to the way the shift towards pop affects some genre conventions. The third mode—the dance musical—was, as we shall see, less established and it took some time for audiences and producers to embrace it as part of the tradition. But first, I will closely consider the circumstances that allowed this merging between the pop music industry and Hollywood.

Even at the end of the seventies, reservations regarding pop's potential to be part of longer narrative structures were still strong, even if they were based on a blanket anti-pop bias rather than experience.[3] But sometimes the reasons for resistance were more technical and had to do with intrinsic aspects of the rock approach to song. In a chapter that focuses on how the rock grooves marked the end of the traditional Broadway musical, Richard N. Grant explains that such limitations are essential to the aesthetics of pop and especially rock.[4] Some of the initial objections to the alleged failure of pop music to provide tools for storytelling became less acceptable as pop explored new styles. For instance, the idea that pop was by nature simplistic did not hold up as the sixties progressed. True, in 1964 pop was dominated by the bouncy, avowedly trivial sounds and lyrics of Motown, and the early styles of the Beatles and the Beach Boys, all aimed at teenage audiences. But by 1969, pop music had diversified to reach all kinds of audiences and encompassed a broad range of styles. No longer simply "teen" music, pop music had evolved, and gained substance and a sense of experimentation. As rock and roll producer Sam Phillips predicted in 1959, traditions such as folk, rock, and country, which had been perceived as different, all merged, and voices multiplied while engaging with broader areas of experience, including race, sexuality, drugs, and even with different political ideals and non-western philosophies.[5]

Historians illustrate the progress of pop with the 1967 release of the Beatles' *Sgt. Pepper's Lonely Hearts Club Band*, conceived as "an album," or, more to the point, a "work." So far, pop songs had tended to be marketed as independent items. The consolidation of the album as an independent entity provided a platform to articulate songs as part of something bigger. *Sgt. Pepper* worked as a plotless storybook, pop art rather than dramatic structure, with vignettes in different styles which contributed to something akin to a collage. It's as if it was the equivalent to an "evening's entertainment" that led to revues or vaudeville with a loosely planned playing order. In this sense, it is with "works" (as opposed to mere "collections") such as *Sgt. Pepper* that pop achieved critical credibility. Thematic developments were also paramount. Few songs in *Sgt. Pepper* are standard "love songs" as the ones featured in early Beatles' albums, and some have quite obscure subjects. Besides, an increasing appreciation for stylistic variety was apparent by the mid-sixties, with audiences accepting a broader repertoire of styles. Through *Sgt. Pepper*, listeners were reminded of circuses, vaudeville, marching bands, and eastern sounds. The vocabulary of pop did not just become more complex, it spoke in several tongues, their sounds influencing each other or clashing dramatically.

Although innovative by itself, it must be added that for some mature listeners *Sgt. Pepper* was, in fact, a *betrayal* of what they took to be essential aspects of rock, and some hardcore fans turned to groups such as the Rolling Stones as a result: by attempting "art," the Beatles were abandoning "realness."[6] It was at this point that the lines between "pop" and "rock" were drawn, authenticity became a central mythology of rock, and audiences as well as critics were forced to take sides. The Beatles weren't alone in their explorations: many performers, even when occasionally identifying their music as rock, were consciously moving into new directions, either reinterpreting the legacy of rock or abandoning some of its essential traits. The Who introduced the intriguingly oxymoronic concept of "rock opera," which combined the raw and the sophisticated, the low and the high. Others dismissed both the intellectualism and the obsession for authenticity in pop music and were happy to go along with the shameless commercialism of the Supremes. And in those heady years, a new awareness for the pop past encouraged some groups or individuals to re-assess the legendary times of *rock and roll*, and to interrogate them, in an attempt to update what was revolutionary about that style. In another line of development, Bob Dylan showed that lyrics could be poetic, allusive, and complex to an extent that songs in popular entertainment, such as movies or TV, could not afford to be, and he consistently resisted labels for his work. He became a divisive presence in the pop landscape. Then there was psychedelia, that took as its inspiration the effects of drugs, and by the end of the decade soul became a well-established genre label. Recordings produced by the wildly commercial Motown were increasingly less reluctant to express "race" in political terms (culminating with Marvin Gaye's 1972 "work" *What's Going On*). At the same time, David Bowie took inspiration from psychedelia, Marc Bolan's glam and camp theatrics, and science fiction to produce *Space Oddity*. Although the album was not a success initially, he continued experimenting with these elements and he came up with a new persona, Ziggy Stardust, in 1972.

Rock continued to be praised as an ideal by the specialized press,[7] as discussed in the introduction, but even music that embraced the label was not consistently written in a particular style or inspired by consistent themes. Pop now provided a whole matrix of moods, styles, and images, which amounted to a lexicon which could be used expressively. Most importantly, every strand of pop expression brought to the table different inflections on race, sexuality, social awareness, and aesthetics. Just the right materials to tell a story. All of this can be recycled into drama: the conflict between approaches with competing agendas, the differences in mood, the variety of voices.

New stylistic repertoires, which consolidated between 1967 and 1972, meant that pop was more likely to provide structure, characterization, and variety. Organizing these elements to engage with the established musical was the next obvious step. But a shift was also needed to bring the different business dynamics of pop music and Hollywood close enough to work together on film, a way to bridge the gap between records and feature films. Few individuals influenced this convergence as much as producer Robert Stigwood. Although some of his efforts within that formula flopped (most notably the films *Sgt. Peppers Lonely Heart's Club Band* and *Staying Alive* [1983]), others were watershed moments in the use of pop music for feature films: *Jesus Christ Superstar* and *Tommy* were Stigwood properties that transitioned from recordings or the stage to screen under his supervision, and he caught the disco trend as it boomed to produce *Saturday Night Fever*. Stigwood came to London from Australia in 1960, in time to become a music man by discovering young pop singers. Although not always discerning or elegant according to certain sources (accounts present him as ambitious, unprincipled, somewhat shady, tenacious, and more concerned with business than with the aesthetic qualities of the musical material), he moved successfully through a world of agents and performers.[8]

Besides his drive towards controlling all aspects of the business—from discovering and grooming new performers to developing careers and producing and marketing events—he had an interest in the theatrical, which is a way of saying he was interested in the way music, records, and concerts developed storylines with a dramatic impact. So he was among the first to believe in the "rock opera" as a notion. He encouraged the creation of the Who's *Tommy*, the first self-labelled "rock opera." *Tommy* is about a traumatized kid who becomes a rock idol and his parents take advantage of his success. There is hardly any dialogue, just songs. It could play as a musical or as a rock concert and, with a substantially reworked plot, it became a film in 1975. As an example of Stigwood's strategic synergy, the film version of *Tommy* starred Roger Daltrey and benefited from the presence of rock stars in small roles, including Eric Clapton, Tina Turner, and Elton John. To turn it into a reasonably cogent "opera film" in 1975, Ken Russell had to strengthen the narrative throughlines which were only hinted at in the original concept album. The film version of *Tommy* is still fragmented and not a fully logical narrative: Strong characters like the Acid Queen, Cousin Kevin, and the Pinball Wizard appear out of nowhere, perform their songs and then disappear, revue-style; scenes are built around songs with no logical connection between them; some turning points are not effectively explained; and characters are not always consistent (it is difficult to know what we are to make of Tommy's mother, for instance). It was, however, very successful. Similar accommodations were necessary for other early rock musicals.

Later, Stigwood would be credited with the introduction of synergy in 1970s musicals. This notion is not as straightforward as it might seem. A certain approach to synergy had always been a part of musical films: Hollywood had consistently used pre-existing stars, from Fred Astaire or Al Jolson to Ricky Nelson, in order to promote their product, and they had counted on hit songs and record sales for extra revenue which brought extra profits to the stars through exposure. Beyond this, Stigwood's role was to identify the ways in which certain products could benefit from pop marketing strategies and styles. Never a "filmmaker," Stigwood however represents, like some of the early moguls of Hollywood studios, a keen-ness for the final product and an awareness of how certain elements could work together.

As we can see, the embrace between pop traditions and the Hollywood musical required some give and take, however the process would be com-pleted in the mid-seventies. The rest of this chapter is concerned with such negotiations between the demands of pop music and those of the feature film, and in focusing on the post-1975 period, it deals with the convergence rather than the incompatibilities between these two industries.

Rockin' Integration: The Rocky Horror Picture Show
and Moulin Rouge!

As the seventies progressed, some musicals signaled a new confidence in the possibilities of pop-driven musical storytelling. *The Rocky Horror Picture Show*, following *Jesus Christ Superstar* and *Tommy*, remains one of the most popular musicals ever,[9] and is a good example both of the new attitudes that consolidated the pop musical and the embracing of pop styles. The original stage musical, *Rocky Horror Show*, originated at the Royal Court Theatre Upstairs in London, where it opened in 1973. It was a cheeky send-up of B movies (as referenced in the opening song) with touches of underground cabaret, wittily laced with the semantic elements and the worldview of glam rock, then at its peak of popularity. After a hugely successful run on the stage, the show was adapted for larger houses; it was a hit when it transferred to Los Angeles but failed on Broad-way in 1975. The film version had already been commissioned at this point, just as glam rock, one of the play's aesthetic inspirations, was in steep decline (it would be succeeded by punk as a "new" style in the fol-lowing year). In that sense, the film remains as a faint echo of a once prominent sound, but also marks a new deal with its audience. Jim Shar-man, the director of the original production, was assigned to direct the Fox-produced film version in the same year. It was shot very quickly, but after the Broadway experience, the studio had lost confidence, put little effort into promotion and early release prospects looked poor. The critical response was muted at best and often downright hostile.[10]

Reviews were not kind,[11] and even a tribute volume which gathers testimonies from everybody involved in the film insists on how "bad" the film was.[12] Almost immediately, however, *The Rocky Horror Picture Show* acquired cult status. It went into the midnight cinema circuits in New York and later became a staple of the exhibition repertoire everywhere, becoming one of the longest running general release films in history. These midnight screenings had been going on for a few years by 1975, and always attracted a young countercultural crowd.[13] The experience of being there among a like-minded audience counterbalanced the lack of a fully coherent film narrative. The progress towards the convergence between the Hollywood musical and pop was driven by changes in spectatorship. Soon, audiences were repeating campy lines and interacting with the screen. Examples such as *Song of Norway* (1970) or *Doctor Dolittle* (1967) suggest that the more traditional musical was, in general, losing contact with the reality of the times. *The Rocky Horror Picture Show* is not just a pop musical, it was a pop cultural *event*, that encouraged countercultural attitudes, addressing a specific, real audience. This points towards a blurring of the limits between the screen and the audience that is similar to the blurring between stage and auditorium encouraged in pop concerts.

Rocky Horror's storyline is gleefully cliché-ridden. Brad and Janet (Barry Bostwick and Susan Sarandon), two naïve youngsters, are caught up in a rainstorm and then their car breaks down in the vicinity of an old dark house; they seek help, but are quickly swallowed up by a party involving outrageously dressed individuals. Their host, who immediately invites them to "spend the night" (that's a hint!), is "transvestite from transsexual Transylvania" Frank 'n' Furter (Tim Curry), and the cause for celebration is the "birth" of a beautiful "creation" he intends to use as a sex object. A series of frantic complications involving erotic antics follow, culminating in a staged revue in front of an empty auditorium in which Frank states his liberational creed, only to be stopped by his two servants bearing orders from extra-terrestrial authorities commanding him to go back home and put an end to his party games.

Since its release, critics have pointed out that the plot is not always logical or that it does not flow smoothly. Although the songs are written specifically for this dramatic scenario, they sometimes appear generic:

"Hot Patootie" contextualizes the character of failed "creation" Eddie rather obliquely, but does not explain where he's come from; and "Rose Tint My World" is not exactly the kind of lyric that clarifies the moment in which it is sung during the cabaret section. But somehow the absurdity works on another level, indulging in the qualities of a pop concert even to a greater extent than *Jesus Christ Superstar* or *Tommy*. Glam rock was always about artificiality, and important strands of pop music emphasize the distance between songs and the real world: a gap that traditional musicals had attempted to close through more conversational lyrics and songs. The pop sound in the songs for *Rocky Horror* reinforces the distance between style and the world, challenging any expectations of realism or plausibility. The fact that the film nowadays is often exhibited in an "audience participation" mode, which blurs the limits between the screen and the audience, contributes to this effect.

The way elements of traditional integrated musicals coexist with glam rock is not very consistent, but a full understanding of the film requires some awareness of the glam rock movement's implications. The more specific parallels between Frank 'n' Furter and Bowie's Ziggy Stardust become apparent towards the closure of the film, with the former's demise as a victim of conventionality. Even more importantly, the film's message reflects glam rock's artificiality against rock's "authenticity." If the latter saw rebellion as violent conflict and a return to nature expressed through chaos, primal screams, and raw behaviour, for glam rock, rebellion arises out of aesthetics, costuming, and artificiality. Glam rock began as an expression of discontent against a trend in rock styles of the late sixties, a turn away from the machismo of traditional rock.[14] Both its ethos and its aesthetic surfaces were perfectly captured in Richard O'Brien's original stage show, which provided many occasions for dressing up and looking back. In glam rock we have an example of a style in which certain signifiers (feather boas, fishnet stockings, make up, glitter, gothic imagery, ray guns and other science fiction paraphernalia, sequined costuming) are used to convey a theatrical, gender-bending ethos. As a consequence, Frank's invitation during the revue show to "be" rather than just "dream," claims artificiality both as liberation and as a way of life, thus conveying a particular version of counterculture. With glam rock, the film also brings into the musical some of the more modern concerns outlined in the introduction: the body, identity, and sexuality are all presented in non-traditional ways (figure 2.1). The male

Fig. 2.1: Corsets, fishnets, and camp. *The Rocky Horror Picture Show.*

body is objectified, identity is flowing and presented as undecidable, sexuality is not disguised through romanticism. A pansexual orgy as a plot event
had been unheard of outside porn, and Frank's funny, outrageous pursuit of
Rocky's minimally costumed flesh during the number "Sword of Damocles"
was among the strongest depictions of male-to-male desire in mainstream
cinema at the time.[15]

   In terms of the way musical numbers relate to the plot, we also see the
coexistence of pop and the "integrated" dynamics of the post-1940s
Broadway musical. Most numbers are written as showtunes, often doing
the work they would do in a Rodgers and Hammerstein musical: the characterization, making dramatic points, establishing the premise of the
story. After the MC (an "Usherette" in the original, represented by huge
red lips during the credits in the film adaptation) introduces the mood of
the film, Brad—prompted by the wedding of some friends—declares his
love to Janet in a jaunty rock song ("Dammit Janet"); later, the characters
express their hopes for assistance at a house they see in the distance
("There's a Light"). These are both typical "I wish" songs: a convention of
integrated musicals. The atmosphere at the house is established through
the "Time Warp" (fulfilling the function of describing a location), then
Frank introduces himself (characterization), and later voices his desire

("Charles Atlas") etc. The styles referenced are commensurate to character. So, the numbers for the couple, are closer to the sound of traditional showtunes ("Dammit Janet," "Touch-A, Touch-A, Touch Me") or soft rock ballad ("There's a Light"): the more naïve characters sing in the more old-fashioned styles, although their numbers become edgier as they lose their innocence. Besides, the musical numbers illustrate and mock a non-traditional romance: characters start as naïve and wide-eyed but end up tarnished and more sexually knowing. "Hot Patootie" is a number for biker Eddie (played by rocker Meatloaf in the film): a "failed experiment" of Frank 'n' Furter's who bursts out of a freezer where his disappointed creator had locked him up. Eddie's song is a key moment in the film, as it suggests a sense of waste, of hidden forces that glam rock has had to repress. It is also a nostalgic gesture: originally titled "Whatever Happened to Saturday Night," it was about simpler pleasures and less complicated lives not too distant in spirit to Don McLean's "American Pie."

It was on film that *Rocky Horror* reached its full impact: somehow the show needed to engage with the traditions of Hollywood onscreen and needed some Hollywood paraphernalia to reach its full potential. The imagery references science fiction B movies and old musicals, and there is a literal revue performance towards the end. The utopian focus is represented in terms of queer sex: Frank, Rocky, Columbia, Brad, and Janet share a blissful orgy in a pool which references the Esther Williams MGM aqua-ballets and is presided over by an RKO tower. When Frank is shot down by the other aliens, Rocky rescues him in a way reminiscent of the RKO film *King Kong* (1933). The conventions of the musical are there as well: the song "Don't Dream It, Be It," sang by Frank during the final performance, links the show to the utopian aspirations of the Hollywood musical as it did in some "11 o'clock numbers" which were planned as final character statements towards the end of shows.

Integration of song and plot was not at the center of pop musicals for the following two decades. There were some outliers, such as *Grease* and *Little Shop of Horrors*, but both were initially marketed through their styles or their success on stage. It took some time for an original plot-integrated pop musical to become a considerable hit. *Moulin Rouge!* seemed to come out of nowhere in the first year of the new millennium. Once again, and despite hits like *The Lion King*, *Dirty Dancing*, and *Evita*, the musical was considered "dead" and as usual the film was hailed as a rebirth of the genre. Director Baz Luhrman had been experimenting with musical form in his previous films *Strictly Ballroom* (1992) and *Romeo and Juliet* (1996).[16] In 1991, he also directed a stage version of Giaccomo Puccini's *La Bohéme*, which rehearsed some of the looks and the sensibility he would develop for *Moulin Rouge!*. The plot for *Moulin Rouge!* has elements of the loose narrative from Henri Murger's literary work, *Scenes of Bohemian Life*; Murger's text was also inspiration for *La Boheme*, which in turn was one of the sources for the Broadway pop musical hit *Rent*. Another starting point is of course the famed Paris dance hall already featured in three important films: *Moulin Rouge* (1928 and 1952) and *French Can Can* (1955). Luhrman borrows liberally but not very precisely from all three films.

Moulin Rouge! is a fitting example of how pop finally influenced musicals without jettisoning some of the genre's central elements. For instance, the double focus that characterizes earlier musicals is presented boldly: the film's plot mirrors this traditional element so closely it could have been put together using Rick Altman's delimitation in *The Hollywood Musical* as a guide. *Moulin Rouge!* sets up an opposition between, on the one hand, the "ideals" of bohemia, and on the other, the sensual fun of show business represented by the Moulin Rouge. The whole plot is organized around the opposition between these two attitudes to life, which is pointedly expressed by the location of the bohemians' quarters across from the opulent, tacky Moulin Rouge. These two sets of principles overlap exactly with the two protagonists, each representing the best about their side of the split: Christian (Ewan McGregor) is sensitive, idealistic, and thoughtful, and Satine (Nicole Kidman) is presented as a beautiful, alluring woman, earthy and ambitious, and who would do anything to achieve success. The plot is well known. A poet moves to Paris's bohemian Montmartre borough in pursuit of his ideals and falls in love with the beautiful Satine, a courtesan and performer in the nearby *Moulin Rouge!*, who is secretly consumptive and, as it transpires, has not long to live. Unfortunately, a wealthy count also wants her, and is willing to invest in the show that will make her into a star if she is good to him. Although she has also fallen in love with Christian, she realizes it is best for everyone if she gives up on her love in order to save the show, and so she sends the poet away. On opening night, Christian walks in and Satine chooses him, but the strain proves too much for her and she dies. The neatness of the structure suggests irony in the film's treatment of genre conventions.

At the heart of the story, Luhrman insists, is the myth of Orpheus: a poet in love with a woman who is trapped in the underworld whom he can't rescue from its pull. As we can see, none of these influences or plot developments are what one would have associated with pop music. Still, such a successful marriage between a "high culture" myth and "low culture" pop is one of Luhrman's achievements in the film. Initially, he attempted to locate the story in a contemporary setting, something resembling the famed Studio 54 disco, but then he thought that rather than avoiding the incongruity between classical themes and contemporary sounds, it would be better to embrace it.[17] It was a carefully devised proposal, as several interviews attest, and clearly Luhrman was concerned about how to produce a new kind of musical while acknowledging his debt to the tradition. Central to the project was the idea to update the connotations that bohemia and the Moulin Rouge had at the end of the nineteenth century, and this necessitated musical styles that would speak to contemporary audiences. As for the songs, Luhrman explains that he took inspiration from classical musicals for where to place them within the narrative. In choosing a mix between a few original themes and a range of pop classics, he's not doing anything very different to what Arthur Freed does with *Singin' in the Rain* (1952), which is mostly made up of old songs. The fact that pop classics are used in the context of 1900s Paris has also been linked to a tradition: in *Meet Me in St. Louis* (1944), Luhrman says, a plot about 1904 combines with music styles belonging to the 1940s.[18] From his reasoning, it is clear that previous knowledge of the songs used and their contemporary sound are essential to the project.

In a bold move, the can-can musical style is transformed into a mashup of Labelle's "Lady Marmalade" and Nirvana's "Smells Like Teen Spirit." Most of the songs used in *Moulin Rouge!* were pop hits,[19] but their use is not consistent and their integration, as these two cases suggest, is not primarily at a narrative level: reading the period's sensibility through a more contemporary one is almost as important. Among Luhrman's boldest moves in this sense is the introduction of a medley of love songs (known as "The Elephant Medley" as it takes place at the top of Satine's elephant-shaped quarters). The characters converse about love and express their viewpoints (Christian is idealistic, Satine is cynical) through short lines from popular pop songs, including David Bowie's "Heroes," Dolly Parton's "I Will Always Love You," and Jack Nitzsche's "Up Where We Belong," among others. Their words are therefore second hand, as with everything else in the film, but they still forcefully express meaning about these specific characters and their situation. However, the scene's exhilaration is also created by the panoply of musical styles and points of view. Interestingly, this song, one of the most effective moments in a pop musical, is predicated on a dismissal of rock "authenticity": pop is used as a collage of voices.

At least since the seventies, the musical had attempted to outgrow the set of common places proposed in the film: most examples studied in this book depart from the conventions of the classical musical far more than *Moulin Rouge!*. One could say that what made the film so unusual in 2001, was precisely the shameless use of the classical musical tradition in the narrative combined with a fiercely contemporary sensibility. It proved that there was nothing like pop music to make old clichés come alive.

Something to Dance About: Three Dance Musicals

Popular music has always maintained links to specific dance cultures. In the 1920s, for instance, jazz bands played in dance halls as background music for social gatherings. Pop music has also gave rise to its own dance cultures: besides listening records, pop music as a social practice entails dancing to those records. This will be reflected in the way cinema would integrate dance. This strand within the pop musical focuses on dancing, often with social implications, pushing song lyrics to the background. The classical musical had also included dancing, often very prominently, but song used to be the defining trait of the musical film: traditional showtune lyrics could be very articulate, urbane, witty, and often rich in characterization. Songs were of course more marketable than dances: they could be broadcast and covered by different performers, which gave them added value in generating business. One could have song without dance, but examples of dance without a song introduction are far less frequent. A musical number was expected to originate with a diegetic song, rather than just movement, and convey its meaning or its key information through the words and music.

Even if dance had been an integral part of the Hollywood musical from its earliest days, it tended to follow the practices of the popular stage as opposed to focusing on the social activity of dancing. Dance was consigned to the professional side of the stage. In some early instances, dancers just posed in synchronicity to the music or in other, follies-inspired productions, geometry was more important than actual dancing. The Busby Berkeley cycle proposed an approach to dance based on camera placement, composition, and camera movement along with bodies forming patterns. One outcome of this was that camerawork imposed itself over some of the purer qualities of choreography: elegance, the triumph of technique over the limitations of the human body, the inventive interpretation of music. Just as the Warner Brothers' cycle peaked, another group of films at RKO, which would have a great impact on the movies and on culture at large, was on the rise. Fred Astaire, the star of this cycle, is still, in the twenty-first century, regarded as a milestone in our understanding of dance.

In her book on dance in film, *Dance Me a Song*, Beth Genné traces a genealogy of dance in the cinema through the different styles that converged in the early 1930s. Astaire remains the great innovator, the performer who put dance at the heart of the Hollywood musical. He is presented as a careful, tireless worker, who rehearsed each musical number in detail. Also, he broadened the possibilities for dance by absorbing influences from ballroom dancing and classical technique, but also from jazz and Black dancers. The Astaire approach to musical numbers is the opposite to Berkeley's: little editing, full-body framings, long takes that focus attention on the elegance, expressivity, or talent of the dancers. Astaire put the dancer at the center of the number.

Film choreography since Fred Astaire partook of moves from "high" and "low" culture. By the 1940s there was a consistent push in the musical towards "prestige," and legitimate dance was an important part of that agenda. Choreographers who started their careers on Broadway and in Hollywood during the classic period often aimed to merge classical and jazz styles of dance.[20] In the pop musical we find a tendency to sidestep classical traditions. Dramatic integration was an important aim in traditional musicals, particularly since the 1940s. Dance had to convey plot elements and needed to work with the narrative rather than just being decorative. Dances by Agnes DeMille or Jerome Robbins were becoming more and more psychologically infused. Although much of what follows will refer to the close relationships between dance and narrative in the pop musical, the traditional approach to integration is not so tightly bound.

Even in traditional musicals, the social implications of dance could not be ignored. And this is one strand in the evolution of the musical that helps us to see some continuity in the genre's use of dance. Whereas Astaire's dances were professional and hardly could be successfully attempted by the average spectator, there was a range of set dances, which could be learnt by imitation. They were publicized in the movies as "the newest dance sensation," and many of these would come and go from the early 1920s. "New Dance Sensations," from the "Charleston" to the "Piccolino," actually just promoted existing styles. The ploy kept customers of dancehalls engaged, and it continued into the age of pop music: the John Waters film *Hairspray* shows how TV was instrumental in making dances known to teenagers. Examples are "The Twist," the "mashed potato," the "frug," the "loco-motion," the "swim," and several Latin rhythms like the "cha cha cha" or "la bamba." Although the interest in dance styles petered out in the mid-1960s as pop became more about the songs, it resurfaced in the 1970s with the rise of disco. *Saturday Night Fever* fits into this context: it updated the "new dance sensation," extending the showcase of a particular style to a whole film. As *The Rocky Horror Picture Show* did a couple of years earlier, this is an example of the musical as a genre interacting with social trends. In fact, a case could be made that it was a key title within the evolution of the genre, as it foregrounded the kind of dance which audiences recognized as their own whilst song was pushed to the background. My other two examples of dance musicals build on this idea: the early 1980s break dancing cycle, represented here by *Beat Street*, brought social awareness to the cinema and underlined folk potentialities, and *Dirty Dancing* worked as a traditional musical by expressing its main narrative throughline to danced music.

Producers at Paramount hesitated to market *Saturday Night Fever* as "a musical." More than ten years of hit and miss attempts (for every hit such as *Funny Girl* there seemed to be several flops, such as *Sweet Charity*, *At Long Last Love*, or *Lost Horizon*) had not only given the genre a bad commercial reputation but also old-fashioned connotations that clashed with the fiercely contemporary pleasures of disco, John Travolta, and the

Bee Gees. This project of producer Stigwood's was shamelessly current, and some critics accused him of just cashing in on what was considered a cheap commercial trend.[21] Still, it is interesting to note how much in the story and in the use of musical numbers falls within the Hollywood musical tradition but is also laced with seventies angst identifiable with the New York of that time. In fact, the origin of *Saturday Night Fever* is a magazine feature by Nik Cohn, "Tribal Rites of the New Saturday Night," on the obsession with discos in working-class neighborhoods. This anthropological element is perfectly articulated in the diegesis. In a canny move, Barry Keith Grant studies this film alongside *West Side Story* (1961), as two films that feature New York City as a "real" place.[22] Fifteen years apart, their differences suggest the new potentialities opened up by the pop musical when making the social dimension of film even more prominent. *West Side Story* owes much to the post–Rodgers and Hammerstein traditions in dance and attempts to bring them to the street but, despite the crucial choreography of Jerome Robbins in three dance numbers, still relies on song.[23] On the other hand, *Saturday Night Fever* leaves these conventions behind. Dance is not so psychological, song is not integrated in the classical sense: the film seems to move the formula into an even more bluntly realistic territory typical of other films of the seventies. As in *West Side Story*, *Saturday Night Fever* opens with shots of New York City, soon focusing in on Brooklyn where the characters live. Manhattan, just across the bridge, remains a utopian space where the problems of a working-class neighbourhood can vanish. The film is about the tension between finding ways to stay in Brooklyn and escaping it to accept the responsibilities of adult life. Besides the dancing and Travolta's charisma, urban audiences were bound to relate to the gritty textures and dirty realism of the film, which made the contrast between everyday experience and the nights at the disco even sharper. New York Latinos did not dance like the Sharks circa 1961, but some Brooklyn Latinos in discos expressed themselves through dance in ways very close to the Latino couple in *Saturday Night Fever*. The disco moves were originally a folk tradition with no inspiration from "classical" dance, adaptations of spontaneous bodily contortions when electrified by music, something raw that did not really belong to "culture."

The plot contains a number of clichés straight out of traditional show business mythologies. We have a young, charming, and talented protagonist, Tony Manero, who works at a hardware store, who is explicitly depicted as easy-going but trapped in a very unexciting life, living in a modest, conservative Italian American household with his quarreling parents. He has no qualifications and seems to be condemned to stay at his job forever. His only moments of joy come when each Saturday he goes to the disco, where he becomes a star of the dancefloor. The story follows some key plot points in the rising star narrative: The character has ambition; he expects his talent to be recognized by winning a competition; he must go through certain hurdles, like choosing a partner or overcoming his own mental obstacles; and finally he wins the competition. Travolta's partner seems to be a detour in the plot: Stephanie (Karen Ann Gorney) is a snotty young woman who works at a record company in Manhattan, who initially looks down on Manero. He describes her talk as "bullshit": she's all about adopting the aspirations of his wealthier friends and employers across the river, and escaping a world defined by "tribalism." The set-up has echoes of the Astaire-Rogers relationship (at one point, Manero is explicitly compared to Astaire) and they similarly come closer together through their dancing partnership as they rehearse for a competition. In an unexpected twist, Manero will give up the award they have won in a climactic competition, as he considers the Latino competitors were clearly superior (but were victims of racist bias): beyond the showbiz mythologies, this film has a seventies awareness of reality and of moral choices. The climax is no simple *celebration* of talent. Even at its most frivolous, there are moral dilemmas within the dancing contest and the world of the disco is not completely isolated from reality. Again, the comparison with *West Side Story* is useful: in the latter, the end expresses a utopian drive towards ironing out differences (i.e., erasing "the social"), but for Travolta, what the film proposes as a precarious utopia has to be left behind and there's no clear solution.

Although not an "integrated" score in a traditional sense, the songs' words underline some elements of the diegesis. The lyrics to the opening credits song "Stayin' Alive" are heard as we see our protagonist Tony Manero strutting down the street: "Well you can tell by the way I use my walk, I'm a woman's man, no time to talk." Although there are some connections between the lyrics and the character, the characterization is misguiding as the film will develop its portrayal of Tony in a different way. At best, the song obliquely expresses the way he sees himself or conjures a character he might identify with. Later, "Disco Inferno" is a conventional song used to set up the space of the 2001 Odyssey *discotheque*, with words that do not help us to understand what the place means for the characters, or within the film's logic. And the dreamy "More Than a Woman" suggests that Tony is falling in love with Stephanie and provides a comment on his state of mind, though even the diegesis is ambivalent about it and does not fully support the words. Although there are "musical numbers" in the film that roughly have equivalence in conventional categories of the musical, neither of the aforementioned examples have characters bursting into song, or crossing over into fantasy worlds. The musical numbers are in smooth continuity with the plot, and sometimes they don't have clear beginning or ending points (they feel casual rather than organized as proper numbers). In that sense, the flow between musical moments and non-musical ones in *Saturday Night Fever* mimics the way one moves from one to the other in life, thus providing smoother transitions than in the clearly marked beginnings and endings of classical musicals. Bursting into song, one of the more extraordinary aspects of the musical genre, and one of the stumbling blocks for non-fans, is not an issue here. The film thus adopts the fluidity between performance and real life, that was identified in the introduction as one of the areas of innovation in the pop musical. As in other examples in this section, the limits of the stage are blurred by the narrative and the mise en scène.

In producing *Saturday Night Fever*, Stigwood had not chosen just any musical style: disco was gleefully escapist, avoiding the (occasionally) serious treatment of race or rebellion that other contemporary styles were hinting at. The songs were eminently danceable, which created opportunities for synergy, and the music style chosen became a hit commercially: *Saturday Night Fever* remains the best-selling film soundtrack ever. Some pop styles went for authenticity, some encouraged mindless joy, and disco was clearly in the latter camp. In the words of Simon Frith: "Disco is, I believe, a rather cerebral form of music-making, certainly in contrast to rock's romantic sentimentality and neediness."[24] Like so much in pop music, disco had origins in Black music, soul specifically, and, as with the original Black inspiration for rock 'n' roll, it went through a process of white mainstreaming, and was also creatively articulated and marketed by gay men. Disco brought back some of the utopian elements of dance.[25] Disco songs are generic, and many of them are just expressions of fun or explicitly named after the place where they were played: "D.I.S.C.O," "Disco Inferno," and "The Best Disco in Town" are examples of a genre that is obsessed with itself. In terms of its implications, Simon Frith emphasizes the sense of "collective euphoria" implicit in many disco songs.[26] In the seventies, disco created a particular urban subculture strengthened by gay liberation and drugs—which were becoming increasingly visible. When these latter implications became too clear, there was a strong kickback, summarized by the "Disco sucks!" campaign, which effectively ended the trend. Later disco-based films, like *Can't Stop the Music*, were failures.

Disco presented the necessary sharp contrast to the grittiness of midseventies New York, and this contrast works to the advantage of the film: continually we are confronted with the harsh realities characters are reluctant to face, and throughout the narrative, issues of class and ethnicity are foregrounded rather than just naturalized. Disco was the ideal pop genre for this kind of story, and it was the right kind of dancing for the moment: it was both a part of the world the characters inhabited, and it also commented on the delusions it created. It was another example of assimilation (or appropriation) of Black culture into the white mainstream, this time starting with elements from soul. And even if disco was chosen for *Saturday Night Fever* because of its commercial potential, the film uses the style ambiguously. First, because it erases from the narrative its Black origins and the contributions made to it from the gay community. Clearly, homophobia and racism are very much a part of the disco-dancing protagonists. This could be something of an alibi for the filmmakers: it reassures the audience while also expressing concerns about their culture. Also, because the main character's arc moves from being accepted as "the king of the dancefloor" to a move away from the disco and all that disco entails. The film portrays maturity as rejecting the world that has Tony's favored disco club, 2001 Odyssey, and its "tribal rites," at the center. In fact, this is a serious challenge to the traditional show musical in which becoming a star is the objective of the characters and their self-realization. The ending of *Saturday Night Fever*, with Tony crossing over to Manhattan and asking forgiveness and friendship from the woman he had attempted to rape, is a rejection of the utopian principles of disco and a denunciation of its lies. Unlike traditional musicals, the film opts for bringing audiences down to earth at its closure. It would be a break with genre logic if characters in a traditional musical denounced show business as a lie. At the same time, it was the musical numbers and the joy of dancing that audiences appreciated: this is a film that says something different to what audiences believe it says. The utopian qualities of dancing are thus acknowledged, but not wholly embraced.

Break dancing is the style that dominates my second example of a dance musical, and provides a different kind of link between dance and the social that is explored in the pop musical. Subsequent to the rise of disco in the mid-1970s, marginalized Black youths in the South Bronx were creating what would become the most culturally important musical style of the late twentieth century. Hip-hop, if considered as a broad culture, is based on four "pillars": MC-ing, rap, graffiti, and break dancing.[27] For rapper Snoop Dogg, rap is not "pop" music, it is a form of "folk" music,[28] an urban equivalent to the Delta blues that was recorded in the 1920s before the style was absorbed by the recording industry. Monteyne's *Hip Hop on Film* discusses the rise of hip-hop in the post-1970s musical landscape, placing the style within very strict social and geographical circumstances. Monteyne focuses on a short cycle of break dancing films from the beginning of the 1980s. These films have remained outside the tradition of the Hollywood musical, both for formal reasons and because they were seen merely as exploitation films that did not merit critical attention. From the mid-eighties rap would evolve into a more explicitly political type of art. By the millennium, however, it had become mainstream, with rappers treated as Hollywood stars and films featuring narratives that could contain the issues raised by hip-hop culture.

Monteyne identifies the origins of break dancing in Black folk traditions and explains the way it produces meaning by bringing the past into the streets. The best hip-hop movies, such as *Wild Style*, *Beat Street*, and *Body Rock* (1984), face a specific social circumstance through dance. Monteyne studies a hip-hop-based cluster of films that were all produced in the first half of the 1980s, before the consolidation of the new, more aggressively politicized phase of rap culture best represented by groups like N.W.A.[29] In the early eighties, as the films suggest, rap was identified with street art and was closer to the roots of show business. Still, it was already developing an aesthetics, an imagery, and an ethos.

Beat Street, released in 1984 at the end of the cycle, is probably the hip-hop musical that best represents the traits identified by Monteyne.

There would be more films on hip-hop and its artists in the 2000s, after the genre's third phase, but this film encapsulates the early spirit of hip-hop discourse. It features all four "pillars" of hip-hop, it is socially aware (that is, the script engages with actual civic issues), and it features actual members of the hip-hop community. In this case, the guest stars include: the female rap trio Us Girls, DJ Kool Herc, Grandmaster Melle Mel, and the Furious Five. Monteyne contextualizes the hip-hop musical by placing it at the heart of social issues in the South Bronx during the 1970s, with an emphasis on urbanism and race. *Beat Street* presents a landscape of condemned buildings with no electricity and previously set on fire by greedy landlords, subway car depots, underground tunnels, families haunted by memories of death by gang violence, and urban decay. In this context, youth cultures made up of mostly Black and Latino males thrive, and music is an important area where subcultures are articulated. As in *Saturday Night Fever*, dancing is an expression of marginal groups, but here it is presented as a triumph of the disempowered, rather than just an illusion.

The film follows Kenny, a hip-hop MC (figure 2.2), his break dancing younger brother Lee, and his Latino graffiti artist friend Ramón, and places them clearly in the historical coordinates that gave rise to hip-hop. Artistic expression—through painting, dance, or music—is central to all three

Fig. 2.2: MC-ing in *Beat Street*.

characters. Kenny lives with his mother and his brother in precarious conditions, but is fully committed to his métier as DJ. Although not a love story, there is a romance plotline involving wealthy City University student Tracy. The class divide is expressed through their relationship, as well as the difficulties in established cultural practice fully embracing hip-hop.

Although there are fewer musical numbers than in other instances of the hip-hop cycle, they all make important plot points: in most of them, there is narratively something at stake that the number precipitates. For instance, a break dancing battle makes teenager Lee a target of the police, and he ends up in jail until his mother claims him. And the musical number at the end of the film is a heartfelt hip-hop tribute to Ramón, who dies in the subway while fighting a competing graffiti artist. And despite the connection between culture, narrative, and dance, the integration of the numbers in the film does not follow the traditional approach that privileges plot development. If we can call *Beat Street* integrated at all, it is because of the prominence of the dances as part of the culture the film represents: dance works as a background that explains the world the characters inhabit. The numbers themselves are shot in simple ways, which can be seen as an application of the Astaire approach within a pop musical context. Break dancing depends on the skill of the dancer for its effects, and an intrusive mise en scène would detract from this display of talent. Still, against Astaire's professionalism, the film features its performers as possessing raw talent and definitively rejecting the values of high culture. Although exploitative to a certain degree, the break dancing films point towards marginalized experiences and the importance of music for creating community ties.

Finally, *Dirty Dancing* balances elements from the folk musical (the camp's staff asserting a sense of community), the fairy tale (the Romeo and Juliet coupling of the protagonists, the camp as "enchanted" kingdom), and the show musical (the preparation of a performance, with a focus on one particular move). As with my other two examples, dance puts the spotlight on a working-class male: expressive dance is portrayed as contagious and it seems to be the prerogative of the underprivileged. It takes place in the 1960s, in a Catskills vacation camp for wealthy New York Jewish families. These vacation camps were used for networking, community strengthening, and matchmaking. There was severe segregation: the staff (often white and working class, but also Latino and Black) were not supposed to mingle, socially or otherwise, with the customers. Teenager Baby (Jennifer Grey) is there with her parents, although her interest is soon focused on the sexy dance instructor Johnny (Patrick Swayze). From the beginning of the film, music is used for characterization. Baby is introduced with two pieces of background music: "Be My Baby" by the Shirelles (in reference to the character's name), and then Frankie Valli's "Big Girls Don't Cry" (which foretells the character's arc in a process of growing up), both helping audiences to understand her background and worldview. She starts the film as an inquisitive and conscientious teenager, defined by the milder versions of mainstream rock. Johnny is later introduced in a precise number which at some point includes the titular "dirty" moves, to the consternation of the middle-class camp guests.

As in previous cases, dance music in the film carries meaning: the qualifier in the title is not, after all, neutral. If the wealthy families are "clean," structured (figure 2.3), and classical, then the dancing in the staff quarters is "dirty," sensual, and slightly disorganized. Johnny is one of the "entertainment" staff: there to keep customers amused, and, it is suggested, that does not exclude selling his body for the pleasure of wealthy women. Dance is presented as a form of self-assertion to escape

Fig. 2.3: Squeaky clean in *Dirty Dancing*.

exploitation. Soon we'll learn he aspires to more original dance steps, showing an ambition not unlike Tony Manero's, which is his best hope to bridge the gap between his lowly status and the world of the wealthy. The contrast between ritualized, classical dance and styles which are more daring and innovative, is a recurring motif in musicals, and is seen later, to hilarious effect, in Baz Luhrman's *Strictly Ballroom*.

The clash becomes even more pointed when inquisitive Baby visits the staff quarters (not minding a notice that forbids this expressly: it is as if Baby is crossing into a danger zone). The color and editing patterns change sharply at this point. Despite the geographical continuity between the camp and the quarters, it does feel at this point like she's crossing into a different world. The service's common room is warmer, thriving with sensuous motion, sweatier, bubbling with the sexier sounds of Latin music. After exchanging looks (note how Baby is the one who gazes first), Johnny and Baby get together briefly for a few erotically charged steps, after which Johnny disappears (figure 2.4). When Johnny's partner Jennifer is unable to make a professional engagement due to a doctor's appointment for an abortion, Baby offers to learn the steps and take her place. The rest of the numbers follow the pattern of dancing in traditional musicals as described by Altman. Dancing leads to love and there are

Fig. 2.4: Getting dirty in the servants' quarters. *Dirty Dancing*.

implications about sexuality that are expressed more literally than in the Fred and Ginger films. After their first hesitant dance together, there follows a class in which Jennifer joins them both, then there is a joyous rehearsal outside of the camp which takes place on a fallen tree trunk, in a field, and finally in the water.[30] After their first performance together, there is something not yet final about their relationship. The film expresses this narratively in the language of dance: the culmination of the number was supposed to be a particular "lift" that Baby does not dare to go for. The meaning here is obvious, and this missing piece is what will be achieved in the film's second half.

The two main dances in the film's second half perform distinct functions, and have contrasting mise en scène: a clear instance of a film attempting to exploit the connotations of music styles, in order to add dramatic tension to the plot. As their relationship becomes passionate, there is an erotic dance which makes use of numerous shots that break up bodies into fragments. The last dance that Baby and Johnny share, to a new ballad which sounds contemporaneous to the film's production, in contrast to the Latin and rock sounds of previous numbers, is also the film's closure and pulls several threads together. It uses a technique closer to Astaire's approach, by maintaining full body shots of the dancers. On the one hand, it is about Johnny "rescuing" Baby from the corner to which her family have pushed her in an attempt to terminate their coupledom. It is at this point, when all hesitations and obstacles have been overcome, that "the lift" can finally happen. But it also allows the dancer to try out his "new" steps. This leads to a musical conclusion in which the staff join the managers and all tensions seem to be resolved through dance. The love between Baby and Johnny contributes to closing the gap between social groups.

After carefully engaging with notions of genre, Feuer concludes that *Dirty Dancing* fits into the tradition of the Hollywood musical, simply taking it in another direction.[31] The fact that Feuer needs to make an argument for it is a sign of the hesitations about the definition of the genre. Songs performed by the protagonists in diegetic situations, with or without diegetic music, are for some audiences an inescapable element of the Hollywood musical. All musical numbers in *Dirty Dancing* happen over a background of pre-recorded music playing in singles or on the radio, and the characters do not sing. Along with *Beat Street* and *Saturday Night Fever*, they show a way forward for the social dimension of popular music: while all three are inspired by the double focus structure of traditional folk, fairy tale, and backstage musicals, characters are integrated into a context that is class defined and reproduces social tension. The utopian elements of dance are both asserted and challenged.

Rocketman *and the Musical Biopic*

As audiences became aware of pop music's past, it was time to start exploring it by zeroing in on the lives of remarkable artists and performers. As it was the case with the dance musical, pop musicals revived a strand that had always been a part of the Hollywood musical canon, even if it had remained outside of the genre's mainstream. The pop musical brings a fresh approach to the biopic, particularly in the way it handles truth and integrates music and narrative, while retaining some elements from the biopic tradition. For instance, *The Great Waltz* (1938), one of the first important musical biopics, includes the now clichéd "inspiration" turning point, as the composer Johann Strauss comes up with the melody for "Tales of the Vienna Woods" by riding through them in a horse-drawn open carriage. This simple plot device will be repeated in many classical musicals and the tradition carries through into pop musicals: it is present in the scene about Queen's inspiration for their song "Another One Bites the Dust" in *Bohemian Rhapsody*. Soon, popular music was also the object of attention, paying tribute to some of its earliest American twentieth-century icons. *Yankee Doodle Dandy* (1942) was an important production that presented the life of George M. Cohan, one of the great American entertainers. It contains a narrative cliché also present in recent musical biopics: the film is framed by a conversation between Cohan and President Franklin D. Roosevelt, that gives the former the opportunity to "tell his story," a structural device that is reproduced in *Rocketman*.

Since the Hollywood musical's early days, certain films have put composers or musicians at their center. Sometimes the films were little more than revue-style tributes (*Till the Clouds Roll By* (1946), on Jerome Kern's work), others fictionalized real lives (*The Story of Vernon and Irene Castle* [1939], on the eponymous ballroom dancers). Although the revue is no longer a substantial part of the genre, the number of pop biopics has been increasing since the 1990s. None of the mid-century performer biopics such as *Jolson Sings* or *Love Me or Leave Me* (on Ruth Etting) were sup-posed to deal with their subjects in a realistic way, they are better under-stood as tributes and commercial ploys intended to get some popular tunes together. When faced with the choice between telling a clear, logi-cal, narratively plausible story or, alternatively, reflecting the complexity of character or experience, earlier music biopics clearly preferred the for-mer. With the rise of the pop musical, such distortion of facts was consid-ered increasingly unacceptable, and audiences expected these films to deal with the more unsavory aspects of reality which had often been pub-licized. This had to do with wider trends: From the 1970s, cinema could present aspects of experience that had hitherto been suppressed; and also the attitude of audiences towards the new pop idols differed from those simply adoring fans of past decades. For instance, the fans now embraced the idea that pop idols were complicated and flawed, as a series of drug-related deaths in the late 1960s would prove. The pop biopic is therefore much grittier than previous examples of the pop musical.

But rather than presenting complex dynamics within show business or featuring psychologically layered individuals, the emphasis in the first instance tended to be on star performances. The earlier pop biopics, and also the country music biopics, are constructed around a film star aiming for a career-best performance: Sissy Spacek, Jamie Foxx, Reese Wither-spoon, and Rami Malek won Oscars for playing Loretta Lynn, Ray Charles, June Carter, and Freddie Mercury respectively;[32] Joaquin Phoenix, Jessica Lange, Gary Busey, and Angela Bassett were all nominated for their turns as Johnny Cash, Patsy Cline, Buddy Holly, and Tina Turner. Other subjects of star biopics include Frankie Valli, Van Morrison, Jerry Lee Lewis, Tupac Shakur, and the rap group N.W.A.[33] As noted, not all musical biopics make substantial contributions to the complexity of the pop musical[34] or make an imaginative effort to combine song with a life and a star image: biopics of Loretta Lynn, Patsy Cline, and Buddy Holly featured comparatively little music, and in other cases involvement from the artists resulted in superfi-cial, uncontroversial treatment (*Bohemian Rhapsody*, produced by, among others, the surviving members of Queen, was criticized for playing down Freddie Mercury's excesses).[35] Also, they tend to be stuck in an early trend of narratives about rock 'n' roll, noted by Sean Griffin, that place the manager as the antagonist who tries to take advantage of an essentially "good" star. The star can be involved in drugs (*Ray*) or sexual scandals (*Great Balls of Fire!*), but they eventually triumph. This pattern is carried through less literal recreations of circumstances of stardom in *Velvet Goldmine* (which gestures towards David Bowie, Iggy Pop, Lou Reed, and other glam rockers), *8 Mile* (inspired by the early years of Eminem, who stars in the film), *The Rose* (allegedly about Janis Joplin), and *Dreamgirls* (an interpretation of Motown which includes anecdotes about some of its performers, particularly Diana Ross and the "lost" Supreme, Florence Ballard). These can be placed within the coordinates established by Lee Marshall and Isabel Kongsgaard for the pop biopic: they introduce the key idea that rather than prioritizing events from a performer's life, the pop biopic deals with the persona, with the myth, with the performer's meaning rather than with facts. Indeed, if traditional show business mythologies were inescapable in the older performer biopics, new rock mythologies, having to do with self-expression and authenticity, are at the heart of the pop music biopic.[36]

For years, most uses of song in pop musical biopics just followed the chronology in which songs were introduced by performers: in most instances, the songs were placed at certain points because they were released, roughly, at the time the narrative was referring to. This creates a parallel line of development in which the story of the rise to success of the performers appears disconnected, thematically, from the contents of their songs. *Bohemian Rhapsody* includes a sequence on the creation and recording of the title tune but does not really engage with the lyrics as relevant to the story of the performers. Key musical numbers in the film more or less follow the group's hits as they happened, but half of the musical content consists of the re-enactment of a legendary performance at the Live Aid concert at Wembley. The cry of desperation in "Somebody to Love" could have been a song about Mercury's personal need, but here it is just an item in the hit parade, introduced at the start of the film as the background music for the singer getting ready backstage.

This approach can sometimes have a stronger narrative impact when the content of a particular song from the performer's catalogue is connected to what the performer represents: in *Straight Outta Compton*, during N.W.A.'s 1989 Riverside Colisseum concert, the group perform the angry "Fuck tha Police" against local government orders, causing a riot which is used effectively in the plot. A new ethos was emerging in hip-hop, angrier and more explicit than the one represented in the mid-eighties' films. The film used this song to reinforce the evolution of the characters. Indeed, *Straight Outta Compton* would not fulfil its agenda without referring to the content of the controversial songs written by N.W.A., the group that best represents the political turn of rap in the eighties. Similarly, in *What's Love Got to Do with It*, Tina Turner's songs, both during her marriage to Ike Turner and later in her solo phase, reflect her development: although very much a catalogue of songs, the soundtrack also establishes some dialogue with the main narrative.[37]

Marshall and Kongsgaard consider *The Doors* (1991), a biopic of Jim Morrison, a turning point in the evolution of the pop musical biopic subgenre. If we look back to biopics of the 1970s and 1980s, it becomes clear that *The Doors* is the first time there was an attempt to convey elements from the group's song aesthetics in cinematic terms. The push towards stronger integration continued from that point. For Jesse Schlotterbeck, a certain use of songs in the pop biopic, based largely on showcasing performers' back catalogues, dominates twentieth century examples.[38] Furthermore, he notes, singing in the earlier pop biopics seems to run *against* the development of the narrative, as there is a disconnect between the individual and the performer. He adds: "With music positioned as an obligation that creates conflict, certain lyrics are sung to fulfil a contract, not because the character identifies with the content at the time of performance." But, he goes on to point out, twenty-first century biopics bring with them a change by providing a semantically tighter relationship between songs and plot, which he explores with examples *Ray* (2004), as well as in *Beyond the Sea* (2004) and *Walk the Line* (2005). In this sense, probably no pop star biopic has made such a conscious effort to integrate songs in order to expand on or clarify star personae as Dexter Fletcher's *Rocketman*, based on the life of Elton John. *Rocketman* was released in 2019, coming soon after the Freddie Mercury biopic *Bohemian Rhapsody*. The latter, which had lukewarm to negative reviews, was nominated for six Academy Awards and won one for its protagonist Rami Malek, playing Freddie Mercury. *Rocketman*, however, received consistently good reviews but no nominations and it did relatively less well at the box office. The studio had warned producer Elton John against showing explicit content about sexuality and drugs, as it would impact the box office negatively, but the singer claimed that the film would not be an interesting account of his life without those elements. It is by establishing a connection between those dramatic elements and the songs that *Rocketman* integrates Elton John's songbook into a narrative.

Elton's consistency in working with lyricist Bernie Taupin means the songs can work as a running commentary on Elton's life and career, reminding the audience of the more personal elements possible in art. Songs are not just objects to be marketed by taking in some aspects of an invented image of a singer or group. In *Rocketman*'s narrative, there is an interdependence between a persona, a life, and the songs. And then there are the specifics surrounding the singer's persona, which make him the ideal cinematic subject. Elton's performances have been visually spectacular, his personality has been colorful, and he has gathered a series of other interesting connotations that are present in other star biographies: modest origins, drug taking, unconventional sexuality, exhibitionism, a rise and fall trajectory. Also, he has had a candid attitude towards the darker aspects of his life, such as his relationship with his parents and his agent, his addiction to drugs, and his tendency for stage tantrums, which are all described in his later memoir *Me*.[39] He had been aware (as he writes in his memoir), that an Elton John biography could not be sanitized: those things indeed happened, but then Elton took control of the narrative and provided many details of his life in the seventies, aware of the fascination that this part of his life has had to audiences. Besides the singer's own recollections, the film took as its inspiration Tom Doyle's book about Elton's life in the seventies:[40] one key exponent of the representation of rock and roll as a culture of excess—this representation being one of rock's favourite mythologies, as featured in ironic narratives such as *This Is Spinal Tap* (1984) and *Rock of Ages*. The film's attitude to truth reflects trends in more recent pop musicals towards achieving a selective but truthful portrait without dismissing the narrative conventions that make the life story plausible on film. What matters here is how these conventions are reworked in the musical numbers. Unlike the more linear approach featured in other films, Lee Hall's script attempts a structure that creates a perspective: for example, establishing a distance between the subject and his life in his monologue at the addiction clinic support group, which is presented as a turning point for Elton. Elton stomps into the film in full stage regalia, costumed as a red-feathered devil. As he tells other patients his story, parts of the costume are removed and we get to know the "real" Elton John. For the rest of the film, Hall is still constricted by the demands of the biopic: it has to convey a lot of information and some famous episodes *need* to be included as part of this contract with the audience.

The narrative is framed by the clinic's support group, to which we continually return, and closes with the star achieving sobriety. The film's first move is to put all of the more controversial aspects of Elton's personality on the table: he's a drug addict, a sex addict, a shopaholic, etc. The story he narrates then follows quite closely the path of pop stardom. Born in Pinner, London, to a lower-middle-class family with an absent father and a dominating mother (Bryce Dallas Howard), Reggie Dwight (his original name) shows early signs of musical talent, is supported by his grandmother (Gemma Jones) to cultivate his piano skills, and sings in pubs before joining the band Bluesology. At some point he decides to go solo and adopts the name of Elton John. He meets his lyricist and friend Bernie Taupin (Jamie Bell) through the small label he is contracted to, and shortly after this he finds huge success at the Troubadour club in Los Angeles. We don't need a lot of detail about his rise to stardom (besides the extraordinary success at the Troubadour), but it is at this point that trouble starts with his erratic behaviour and experiments with drugs. In keeping with one of the oldest conventions of pop musicals about performers, his agent (and lover) John Reed (Richard Madden) embezzles money, Elton runs into financial difficulties, and issues caused by addiction and a short temper become more serious, but he keeps on recording hits.[41] At one point, when his life is spiraling out of control, he finally plucks up the courage to attend therapy, which justifies the confessional approach to the narrative structure.

The logic of the songs selected from Elton's catalogue is linked to plot rather than the strict chronology of releases: they illustrate specific moments in the singer's life and add layers of emotion to the relationships portrayed. So "Your Song," first recorded in 1970, appears when Elton and Bernie establish their working collaboration and, as presented in the film, it suggests the depth of Elton's feelings for his friend. With words by Taupin and vocals of course by Elton, there is an ambivalence about whose feelings are being expressed. Also, it is a song about *writing* a song that signifies love. The mise en scène presents the singer improvising the impassioned music that works so well with Taupin's casual lyrics. It is one of the film's best examples of the complex, understated relationship between music and plot that re-reads the original song for specific narrative purposes. It's worth comparing the way "Your Song" works in *Rocketman* to the way it functions in *Moulin Rouge!*. As sung by Ewan McGregor in the latter, it is an expression of personal feelings which is used to bring the central couple together after a very awkward encounter based on mistaken identities. In *Rocketman*, the relationship between Reggie/Elton and Bernie is oblique: "Your Song" is not so much used as an explicit declaration of love, but as a look into hidden, understated feelings. The strategy is repeated several times in the film, as if the songs always reflected Elton's feelings at various different points. So, "The Bitch is Back" contextualizes the spunk of five-year-old Reggie; "I Want Love" dramatizes one of the themes of the film, emotional starvation, tying it to the coldness of his father's attitude; "Saturday Night's All Right" shows a transition between boyhood and young maturity rather than just illustrating the lyric literally; and later, the friendship with Bernie will be further developed, through the placement of "Sorry Seems to Be the Hardest Word" after their near break-up.

"Rocketman," Elton John's 1972 song about an astronaut who feels the intense loneliness of space all around him, becomes very specifically linked to one of Elton's lowest moments, and it is also something of a central theme around which the script develops. The origins of the song are quite generic: Taupin stated he was thinking about the immensity of space and, as with "Daniel," he wanted to establish a link between the sky and the earth through a human perspective. For the film, some of the connotations of the song are set into a new context which reflects a very specific state of mind. During a party, high on drugs and surrounded by people he does not particularly like and does not relate to, Elton dives into a swimming pool, apparently to stage a suicide, and sees his childhood self, playing a toy piano at the bottom (figure 2.5). It is an emotionally charged image that links his current isolation with the particular childhood we have seen him experience earlier in the film. The song then begins, with its mournful expression of someone who is going to achieve something amazing but who feels disconnected from reality and, more pointedly, feels that the people around him do not know him. While this idea is developed through song, it is joined by a number of contrasting images, which present the singer's rescue from the pool, the ambulance, the hospital, his recovery and, eventually, his being placed back on stage

Fig. 2.5: Childhood and fantasy. *Rocketman.*

by the powers that be to keep on performing. Again, a song that on record was touching but general, is given a specific new context where it expands on the character and situation. The idea of isolation is certainly explained at script level, and this could have been just a moment in the script that led nowhere, but the song gives it an intensity and poignancy that would be absent without it. The formal, choreographed actions surrounding the singer in the number also emphasize both the disconnect the lyrics describe and a more particular situation of Elton's at that point in his life.

Rocketman is a useful example of how the pop musical has the potential for integration even working from pre-written material. The consistency of style in Elton John's canon and the ambivalence of Taupin's lyrics makes it possible for Hall to extract elements of meaning that clearly reflect dramatic situations. Of course, integration is not literal. It is not as if the character would say *those* words in *that* situation. Each song is simultaneously the song performed by Elton and a song about a situation. In doing this, the film is part of the pop biopic's move towards further integration, consolidating the emerging trend of the early twenty-first century that Schlotterbeck notes in his article. As discussed in the introduction, integration can contribute a number of elements to musical storytelling. In this case, the song's contribution was to add emotional depth to the relationship between Elton and Bernie. In a broader sense, integration here and elsewhere in the film acts to reinforce the links between numbers and narratives. The pleasures of just watching the star on stage are then complemented by giving the song a reason to exist that works on a different level of the film.

This is, in essence, what all the examples in this section do: musical numbers are not just interruptions in the plot with an indifferent impact on their development. Even if the traditional concept of integration doesn't quite work in *Rocketman* or *Dirty Dancing* or *Beat Street*, as it does with *The Rocky Horror Picture Show* with its songs tailored for dramatic situations, the fact is that the numbers in these films are more than simple spectacular interruptions: they add layers to the narrative, the context, and to characterization.

3 LOOKING BACK

The Pop Musical and the Past

> I want you because you remember.
> —*Velvet Goldmine*

Don McLean's song "American Pie," released in 1971, is one of the earliest sung expressions of a yearning for the pop past. Or, more specifically, a yearning for lost youth in the language of a pop song. The song, which puts old rock 'n' roll at the center of memories of a youth, is about the impact of the news that early rockers Buddy Holly, Ritchie Valens, and the Big Bopper had been killed in a plane crash in 1959, a year after Elvis went into the army and rock and roll lost some of its initial impetus. Placing rock 'n' roll in the context of remembering, conveys the idea of days long gone. Indeed, for the singer who recalled reading the news of the crash as a teen, that was the day that "the music died." Everything that happened after that, the whole of the sixties, could not, in his view, live up to the excitement of the mid-fifties. Nostalgia is a sense of sweet regret for having lost things one never really had. McLean's vicarious troubadour sees the sixties as crazy and eventful, but also inauthentic and lacking in substance. "American Pie" could be about nostalgia for youth, but also nostalgia for the time in which a new music was discovered that could not compare to anything else, a generation-defining kind of music. Music can be the perfect vehicle to convey past moods, to recall the past. Music can also distort, conceal, and re-write the past. The three musicals in this chapter re-visit and reassess the past through pop music. The pop musical has proved an effective way of recalling the past nostalgically but also of pointing out its traps. Simon Reynolds identifies this thread in the early work of Mott the Hoople, Bruce Springsteen, Patti Smith, and other performers in the early seventies who would "make subject matter out of rock mythology, rock's lost promise, rock as salvation and liberation theology."[1] In film, the important watershed title for this mode of musical is *American Graffiti*, released in 1973, and there is a developmental line that can be traced from that point to *Grease*, in 1978, and on to other titles.[2] Along with other musicals identified in the previous chapters, these are yet another sign that pop had reached maturity and that its sophisticated awareness opened up further possibilities for the pop musical.

The exploitation of the past for spectacle and nostalgia has always been one of the salient features of the Hollywood musical. With few exceptions, musicals have always preferred a safe distance towards their subjects and have always found ways to erase the darker forces of the recent past. From the mid-sixties, however, the idea of the past has been taken more seriously in plot terms and also in musical styles. *Cabaret*, both the 1966 Broadway show and the 1972 film, are milestones in this process, using original ways to consistently present and criticize a dark historical juncture through song. Although their sound is unequivocally Broadway, there are hints here and there of Kurt Weill and Mischa Spoliansky too.[3] In essence, this is not too different from the way the songs in *Grease*, *Little Shop of Horrors*, or in *Dreamgirls* refer back to older styles.[4] Weimar cabaret was, if anything, recognizable by a mere minority when the musical opened, whereas soul, as evoked in *Dreamgirls*, has a relevance to the way audiences experience the world. Soul carries within it mythologies which are, on the one hand, better known for most people and, on the other hand, culturally central for specific groups. Besides the nostalgic tribute to a sound, soul recalls a sense of personal experience and communal past. *Grease*, set in a high school during the late 1950s, had to evoke the sounds heard by kids at the time, and *Little Shop of Horrors*, set around 1962, needed to allow for girl groups, doo wop, and old rock and roll.

As we saw in the previous chapter, one of the key reasons pop music has had a unique impact on the musical film, is its potential to address disempowered social groups, initially youth communities, and later, groups treated as ethnic others. Forms of mainstream popular music before the 1960s had been homogeneous and addressed "everybody," whereas folk forms could engage with sub-communities defined by geographical or cultural parameters. Pop music started as a fragmentation of audiences (young/old) and later acknowledged different communities which had not enjoyed mainstream self-expression. This was particularly the case for African Americans, but it also implicated women, queer people, and the working class. Some early forms of rock were consistently confrontational rather than reassuring, and this was later exacerbated by the emergence of punk, hip-hop, and other musical genres of the late 1970s. Although necessarily controlled by the apparatus, pop music has been, starting with its origins in marginalized traditions, the crucible where those communities can elaborate on their own memories, their own histories, their own emotions.

The Pleasures of Nostalgia: Grease

Post-war children who were teenagers in 1955, would reach maturity and embrace the responsibilities of grown-up lives in the early seventies. In between those two points lay the revolutions of the late sixties, which were exciting and challenging for many, often exhausting and just a bit disappointing for others. The escape into nostalgia is explored by Michael D. Dwyer in an essay that historicizes the phenomenon which took form in a range of cultural manifestations from the early seventies.[5] Accounts suggest that the film *Grease*, one very successful, very prominent example of the nostalgia craze, was born as a somewhat cynical project. The film was based on a hit 1972 Broadway musical, which was a transfer from a fringe show put together in Chicago the previous year by Warren Casey and Jim Jacobs. The original show was partly a heartfelt evocation of innocent times, partly a knowing pastiche for post–sexual revolution audiences. The plot structure follows the conventions of the fairy tale musical slavishly: in a "special world" (the Rydell High School), two contrasting characters of opposite sexes meet, like each other, fight, and finally become a couple. The bare bones of the story and the syntax is in principle quite similar to the way Altman describes the operetta *The New Moon* in his book *The American Musical*, which makes *Grease* into a perfect example of "rock operetta."[6]

The whole plot is structured in parallel, through a clash between dual protagonists. After a prologue and contextual set-up, we follow the twin reminiscences of Sandy (Olivia Newton-John) and Danny (John Travolta) in the song "Summer Nights" (figure 3.1) adorned by delighted exclamations from their peers, neatly divided into "male" and "female" groups and caricaturing "male" and "female" experience. Shortly after this, the romancing kids clash, realizing that they belong to different worlds. There is the matter of status: wide-eyed Sandy is a naïve, virginal young girl who is new to the school, whereas Danny is the established leader of the leather-clad, tough-on-the-surface, naïve-on-the-inside T-Birds ("Burger Palace Boys" in the original show). Both characters are inspired by types that are common to films of an earlier era. As one song suggests, Sandy's type is Sandra Dee, the star of the sanitized surf film *Gidget*, but by extension her character can also be associated with the Annette Funicello type in the beach party cycle. As for Danny, he is the "greaser," a character type based on the personal memories of Casey and Jacobs growing up in Chicago. "Greasers" were working-class youths, similar to the characters Elvis played in his first film phase, with elements of Dean and young Brando. Of course, the edges of this character were already softened for the stage show, further pushed into PG-ness by producer Allan Carr's watchful eye, and Travolta's charm did the rest to create an engaging, likeable screen character. The rest of the characters are similarly clichéd, and instantly recognizable to those familiar with the youth films of the late fifties. Rizzo (Stockard Channing), leader of the female gang "The Pink

Fig. 3.1: Conflicting memories. *Grease.*

Ladies," is the archetypal "bad girl," cynical and sexually liberated, although her ballad "There Are Worse Things I Could Do" shows she also has a heart. The rest of the T-Birds are randy and they like cars and rock music. Although, for the film, they also have hearts. Frenchy (Didi Conn), who introduces Sandy to the Pink Ladies, is a bit of a bubblehead. With a heart. And so on.

The film's success owes everything to adjustments made to the original, and these have to do with the producers' use of resources from the pop record business. Carr, perfectly attuned to the sensibilities generated by pop music, was the main driving force behind the project. Early on, he decided the film would be cast with old-time stars, particularly for the smaller parts, but the musical numbers would go mostly to the protagonists, who were played by lesser-known actors.[7] As had been the case with *Saturday Night Fever*, Paramount executives had serious doubts about the project: musicals were considered box office poison and memories of unmitigated disasters such as *Lost Horizon* (1973) and *At Long Last Love* (1975) were not too distant. Carr, however, understood the potential and the times perfectly and was well acquainted with the genre as he had worked with Stigwood promoting the hits *Tommy* and *Saturday Night Fever*. Randal Kleiser was chosen to direct, even though it was his first Hollywood film, after the more established Michael Schultz became unable to commit due to another project. Then again, this is not a director's version of the 1950s: a comparison with the original youth musicals of that time suggests that the ideas that shaped the project came from its producer. Accounts by Tropiano and Robert Hoffler underplay Kleiser's role in the production, emphasizing contributions by cinematographer Bill Butler and choreographer Patricia Birch.[8] In fact, as with many traditional musicals, such accounts present *Grease* as an example of collaborative art in which people with different areas of expertise worked together. Despite the diverse strands of influence in the film (pop vs Broadway, the 1950s as seen from the 1970s, naïveté and knowingness, emotion and parody), the result is highly consistent: sets, songs, performances, costumes, and choreography are all stylized and campy.

Synergy was very much at the heart of the project. The film's soundtrack was put together by Stigwood so that it would become a bestselling album: it had the beefed-up orchestrations of a pop record rather than the less impressive ones in the original cast recording, and it did keep the late-1950s style, but also added a more contemporary credits sequence song. This then amounted to a revision in the implications of the film's title, which—now featured as part of the background music to this animated, introductory opening sequence—meant that "grease" was not so much about class anymore. Following his instinct to increase marketability, Stigwood commissioned Barry Gibb of the Bee Gees to write the title song (and this was sung by Frankie Valli over the sequence). In terms of content, this is unimportant. Not even the Gibb brothers thought much of the song: it was quite vague ("Grease is the time, is the place, is the motion") and it did not fit the film's general style, but it rewrote the title's original meaning by effectively denying its working-class roots and saying that "grease" was just a "word," whose meaning was limited to this particular film. The song gave the soundtrack recording an extra layer, suggesting a more contemporary perspective. Half of the score from the original stage production was jettisoned or simply used as background music, but still it was featured on the album, contributing to the nostalgia-infused project. Some of these songs are just reworkings or a pastiche of types of late-1950s songs, and therefore do not contribute to plot and characterization in any notable way: "Those Magic Changes," "Freddy My Love," "Tears on My Pillow," and "It's Raining on Prom Night" do not refer to events in the plot but strongly place the film within its time. Rather than working on their own terms, the songs make the period come alive more vividly and generally.

The plot points or characterizations that the songs served in the original were also omitted so that the film became more about the central couple, and so new songs were written. Louis St. Louis penned "Sandy" as a rock ballad solo for Travolta, and Newton-John's frequent songwriter John Farrar wrote the Oscar-nominated "Hopelessly Devoted to You" (which sounds like early Lesley Gore) for her and also the final duet, "You're the One That I Want," which replaced a similar number in the original (the rock pastiche "All Choked Up"). The 1955 Oscar-winning "Love Is a Many Splendored Thing" by Sammy Fain underscores the film's prologue as one of the most easily identifiable pre-rock ballads of the fifties (in fact, the film makes a statement by creating a sharp contrast between the string-laden song in the prologue and the rock sound of the title song over the credits) and a doo wop-inspired version of Rodgers and Hart's "Blue Moon," similar to the ones produced by Elvis Presley or the Marcels, is also heard at one point, as they would have been heard at teenage balls during the period. As in *American Graffiti*, the soundscape evokes an overwhelmingly white experience, where uncomplicated melodies and uncomplicated emotions deal with old certainties about love.

The *Grease* shoot coincided in part with *Saturday Night Fever*'s release. Despite some common personnel, no two films could be more different. *Saturday Night Fever* acknowledges the contemporary urban lives of the time, it is gritty, it features death and working-class frustration, it is earnest, it deals with ethical choices, has a bittersweet ending, and takes place in something like the real Brooklyn. In *Grease*, costuming, art direction, and cinematography all work together to produce a sun-drenched utopia where solutions to all problems are guaranteed from the start. The difference between the two Stigwood-produced musicals is best expressed by the performances of John Travolta in both films: realistic and conflicted in *Saturday Night Fever*; and ironic, broad, and cartoonish in *Grease*. In sharp contrast, surfaces in the latter glisten and there is an excess of tidiness in the visuals. Some sets, especially the stagy "Beauty School Dropout" (figure 3.2) and the fantasy segment of "Greased Light-nin' " (figure 3.3), suggest more the look of the classical musical than that of the pop musical. The original stage play had been set in an inner-city Chicago high school and the "greasers" the title alluded to made perfect sense in that context. It was Carr who settled on California as a location, as it had sunnier connotations, which were considered perfect for the

Fig. 3.2: Frankie Avalon follies. *Grease*.

Fig. 3.3: Greasers' fantasy. *Grease.*

project: again, reality was exchanged for more idealized surroundings, a lesson learnt from the old beach party musicals.

As many musicals before it, *Grease* does not aspire to be more than fun. But what makes it work, according to Tropiano, is its ability to recall an idealized past: the fifties as represented here are a fantasy of social and sexual harmony, where the battle of the sexes is conveniently and effortlessly ironed out in the last act. Plot elements and settings are borrowed from past movies, music styles evoke the late 1950s, characters are types. To drive the point home, Frankie Avalon has a cameo as the guardian angel singing "Beauty School Dropout." It was not the only casting coup. The adult cast included veterans Joan Blondell and Eve Arden, both great screen presences with a history dating back to the 1930s. This approach to casting would be repeated in two other Allan Carr projects in the next few years: *Can't Stop the Music* and *Grease 2* (1982). The former had Broadway star Tammy Grimes and fifties actress Barbara Rush, the latter included supporting parts from Tab Hunter and Connie Stevens as teachers, alongside Lorna Luft—who also happened to be Judy Garland's daughter. Such borrowings were extended to other stars whose personae were adapted for the film's purposes: for example, Eve Arden being sardonic and Joan Blondell playing a waitress.[9]

So in one way, *Grease* looked forward by establishing synergies with the pop industry, creating a best-selling pop soundtrack, and starring one bona fide pop star, Olivia Newton-John, together with up-and-coming John Travolta.[10] The film is, like the differently angled *The Rocky Horror Picture*

Show, an important illustration of the full use of pop music for the genre to bring about connotations which were unavailable to traditional musicals. On the other hand, *Grease* looks back to the traditions of the pop musicals in the 1960s by quoting from other key films, stars, and characters. In terms of semantics, it is easy to see the film as a riff on the beach party movies, with similar concerns and character types. The film also shares API youth musicals' sense of utopian kids' communities, with no parents to be seen, no responsibilities to take too seriously, pajama parties, drive-ins, and school balls. Despite this insistence on old-fashioned youth films, the film's sensibilities are rooted in the seventies. Consider how the film's denouement eschews the prudish attitudes of the beach party series (in which sex is always something of a joke and kept off screen), and replaces them with a smart move: making Sandy into a rocker. And even if it vanishes just in time for a happy ending, an unwanted pregnancy is at least suggested.[11]

Setting the Record Straight: Dreamgirls

The impact of segregation in early rock went beyond the limited visibility of Black artists. Often, their songs reached the mainstream through other, white performers. To transition to the mainstream, Black music was required to sacrifice politics, identities, and sounds. In the racist 1960s, Motown was a successful example of such negotiations, which were concealed, following show business logic, by a surface of glitter.[12] Motown presented its triumphs as resulting exclusively from "talent." The company's decline coincided with a wave of revisionist narratives that recuperated such negotiations and called attention to the harsh conditions that surrounded them. The source material for the film *Dreamgirls* participated both in the nostalgia trend and the more politically committed revisionist attitude.

Traditionally, Black representation in mainstream films, as well as in Blaxploitation movies, had reinforced, rather than questioned, ethnic stereotypes.[13] Attempts, not wholly successful, were made to change perceptions from the early 1970s. *Lady Sings the Blues* (1972), the Motown-produced biopic of Billie Holiday, was an important step towards the acknowledgement of race conflict in American popular music. And *The Wiz*, a Black appropriation of *The Wizard of Oz* (1939), opened on Broadway in

1974, with a proudly Black cast and a score infused with soul. Motown bought the rights for the film adaptation, which was released in 1978 starring superstars such as Diana Ross, Michael Jackson, Richard Pryor, Mabel King, and Lena Horne. Although the film was a notorious flop, clumsily directed by Sidney Lumet, it follows the spirit of the original and brings to the screen not just the best of soul culture, but also a degree of social conscience that had been absent in Black musicals so far. The stylized sets represent urban spaces close to Black mythologies, and the musical styles used inflect the story, re-writing it from a Black perspective. In the following decades, a series of biopics about Tina Turner and Ray Charles, as well as the rap band N.W.A., focused on Black experience through the lives of prominent artists. *Hairspray*, both the original 1988 John Waters version and the 2007 film musical adapted from the 2002 Broadway show, developed a story about the very real issue of integration in the Baltimore of 1962. All of these films try, in different ways, to historicize Black experience.

Dreamgirls is a late example of the Black musical that manages to deal successfully with both the evolution of pop music and the way it expressed identity and race issues during the 1960s. Aligning with the myths of the "self-reflective musical," the film features plenty of brash triumphalism, relies on natural talent and proposes a happy ending that seems to erase contradictions without actually doing so.[14] But as with many other pop musicals of the twenty-first century, it also engages with suffering, history, and the less commendable workings of the music business. At least three outcomes for Black talent are mobilized by the film. First, commercial success: expressed in the film as an explosion of glamour and visual excess in some of the later numbers. However, the second, linked, outcome is the mixture of compromise and frustration that this success implies. The raw, soul stylings of lead singer Effie (Jennifer Hudson) are, in the light of market preferences, considered unsuitable for the new girl group, and she is eventually fired in a brutal scene. The third outcome is female solidarity: an aspect that was not as fully developed in the original stage show but is closer to millennial sensibilities in the film.

The starting point for the film is a Black success story. Motown records, which absorbed the recently created R & B label Tamla records, was founded by Berry Gordy in 1960. Gordy came from the Black middle class and had experience working at the Detroit Ford car factory before he decided to go into the recording business. His inspiration was to challenge segregation and ultimately to cross over into the mainstream of the record business. Motown's early years were tough, but by 1962 the company took off, and during the 1960s it became the most important Black-owned company in the United States, as well as one of the most consistently successful entertainment operations in history. The Temptations, Stevie Wonder, Marvin Gaye, Smokey Robinson, Martha and the Vandellas, the Jackson Five, the Four Tops, and, of course, Diana Ross and the Supremes, were some of the main attractions, producing an astounding catalogue of material. In the documentary *Hitsville: The Making of Motown* (2019), Gordy insists on the similarities between Motown Records and the Ford production chain's quality control structures. This is true, but another parallel can be found in the movie studios of the classical era, both as a model for production and in their effort to address "America" by erasing conflict, whether racial or sexual. Production was centrally controlled and supervised to meet standards of quality and consistency. Artists were costumed, trained, and taught everything from dancing to table manners. The result was a very polished output, perfect on the surface, and perfectly trivial at heart.

The original *Dreamgirls* stage show opened on Broadway in 1981. Michael Bennett, working from the script by avant-garde writer Tom Eyen, took up the challenge of balancing the glamour of a Broadway musical with a story specifically rooted in issues derived from segregation. The result was stagy and striking, with a particularly attention-grabbing performance by Jennifer Holliday as Effie, who would go on to win a Tony. Reviews emphasized its formal conception and aestheticism rather than the more historical aspects. The set was particularly praised: it was semi-abstract and consisted of light towers that could be moved and turned around to reconfigure different spaces. The show was also intensely theatrical, and contemporary audiences would recall the gasps elicited by key moments.[15] The original material can be interpreted to propose an idea close to some readings of the Elvis style noted in chapter 2: that "Black music" became a mainstream success by jettisoning its authenticity. Both the plot and the music articulate this idea carefully. However, Nelson George, in his account of the 1980s from a perspective he calls "post-soul," points out a contradiction at the heart of the original: "The irony of *Dreamgirls*' argument about gritty soul music being discarded in favour of insubstantial musical styles is that Bennett's direction is as slick as a pair of spandex pants. His staging is very much a triumph of style over substance."[16] In other words, for George, the fact that the history of racial struggle has been appropriated by white men somehow pushed the importance of historical relevancy to the background.[17] Although this is to some extent also true in the film version, I will argue that for reasons to do with casting and the effects of cultural change between 1981 and 2006, *Dreamgirls* has become an important text to illustrate the tension between mainstream and Black culture.

Despite strong denials that the play was based on the Supremes, the parallels are too many and too shamelessly obvious to miss. The group's manager in the stage show, Curtis Taylor, is a car dealer, and Gordy had also worked in the car industry; the Supremes debuted doing backup with the original stage name of "The Primettes," whereas in the film they are "The Dreamettes;" of course there is the resemblance between "Deena" and "Diana" (figure 3.4); in the film, Effie is fired in 1967, the same year as Florence Ballard was let go and the group was renamed "Diana Ross and the Supremes;" and Ross had an affair with Gordy, who by some accounts was fiercely autocratic and was reportedly involved in payola, at least in Motown's early days. These may seem like cosmetic similarities and they are counterbalanced with other elements that refer to The Shirelles.[18] In other instances, elements from different real-life figures are used: R & B star Jimmy Early is based on Jackie Wilson and James Brown, with a

Fig. 3.4: Diana or Deena? *Dreamgirls*.

performing style that might suggest Little Richard. In the film adaptation the character also echoes Marvin Gaye in aiming for more "socially conscious" music with the newly written song "Patience," which refers directly to late-1960s race riots.[19]

Other changes introduced for the film version also contribute to an increased sense of the historical context. Detroit, home of Motown (and not Chicago, as in the original), becomes the hometown of the protagonists and the place where most of the action takes place. And there is a clear agenda to use layouts and fonts that recall Motown publicity images, costumes and, in general, to strengthen rather than play down the parallelisms, thus providing a more secure historical anchoring. The film also conveys a stronger sense of space and time, by putting great care into its costumes and sets. One result is that the film vividly recreates a period which returns to its audiences as stylish, cool, and glamorous. In a way, this reproduces the emphasis on aesthetics that Nelson George points out about the original. On the other hand, it also contributes to anchoring the film in history: this is less a story about "Americans," as Bennett had implied, than a story of Black American women working in show business and having to deal with an added layer of oppression.

The film's promotional campaign made an attempt to emphasize Black input (based on stars and dancers, as well as choreographer Fatima Robinson), even if, as in the case of the stage original, key positions had been given to white artists. The documentary "Building the Dream," included in the Blu-Ray edition, appears defensive on this issue. Some critics at the time were even more specific, deeming it "a gay man's fantasy on black stars."[20] Others added that despite its efforts, the things the film chooses to represent are not too different from the kinds of things associated with certain stereotypes of race in America: certainly, the film takes a very white approach to "[B]lack realness."[21] Timothy Laurie points out how, in terms of plot, the film falls into stereotyping by making Curtis into the antagonist and characterizing him with elements from historical repertoires ("the Black pimp") that produced a racist view of Black experience.[22] But even if justified by the demands of the plot, the set-up still inescapably creates issues. Again, Laurie:

> While Taylor's DJ payoffs are initially forgivable, his payola network ends up suppressing one of Effie's solo singles when she

tries her luck at a comeback. This twist hinges on a syntactic separation between pre– and post–Civil Rights moral universes: having "stepped to the bad side" in an unjust, pre-integration America, Curtis's use of payola ceases to be defensible by the 1970s, skewing the level playing field upon which Effie would otherwise have scored a first hit. The main social barriers facing the Dreams (and ex-Dreams) shift from racial discrimination to Curtis Taylor Jr himself: as he puts it to Deena, "You can´t even take a shit and wipe your own ass unless I say it's OK."[23]

It's a narrative choice to concentrate on the rise of the girls alongside the businessman as antagonist. The latter was, it must be remembered, one of the tropes of youth musicals. One should wonder, though, whether it remains relevant in a story that purports to engage politically with racism.

These are compromises for the project to reach a wide audience, which mirror the compromises Black artists had to accept in the past to achieve mainstream success. Still, as a musical, it does important work by confronting the segregation in the pop music industry rather than just embracing show business mythologies uncritically. Casting in the film contributes to the film's dialogue with history. The character of Deena is played by Beyoncé. The result of this choice is twofold. The film focuses on a "new," "positive," "powerful" star image that is both linked to and distant from the Diana Ross persona. Jaap Kooijman follows up the implications of such casting by comparing the implications that Beyoncé contributes through her star image to Ross's star image.[24] At the same time, Kooijman adds, as a gay icon, the Beyoncé image could help sell the film to an additional audience. Beyoncé carries an image that is strongly commercial and only subtly political: she could be seen, in the past, to be supporting the Obamas, for example, but she has never made explicit political statements on controversial issues. Beyoncé represents a fantasy of achievement for Black women that works well with the Deena character, set against the newcomer Jennifer Hudson who plays the rougher character Effie. There was a second important casting coup. For Eddie Murphy, playing James "Thunder" Early was both a departure from and a return to his roots. Murphy was the key Black star of the 1980s, the first post-soul decade. In those years, he had contemplated a career as a singer before making it as a comedian via *Saturday Night Live* and starring in a profitable series of comedies for two decades. According to Nelson George, what Murphy contributed to the image of the Black comedy star was a shift away from the more inevitably politicized personae of Richard Pryor or Bill Cosby who had come to prominence at the end of the civil rights era and were therefore linked to it. In following a trajectory that travels from soul to socially conscious ballads, the character Jimmy becomes richer with the reverberations brought on by Murphy, as well as the echoes of Marvin Gaye, which were not present in the original show.

The film's narrative is also critical of the characters' compromises. One of the premises of the *Dreamgirls* plot is made explicit by songwriter C.C. (Keith Robinson) in the film: there is a widespread assumption that "Hound Dog" is an Elvis Presley song, whereas the song was written and introduced by Big Mama Thornton, a Black performer. In other words, the legacy of Black music was often re-appropriated in order to guarantee "mainstream" success.[25] In the film, C.C. pens "Cadillac Car," a song which feeds on the Black fantasy of owning a big automobile as a sign of status. The song does very well for performer Jimmy, and it climbs up the charts until it is covered by the whitest, blondest, teen balladeer and is featured on TV over a background of sandy beaches and palm trees (the original libretto mentioned Pat Boone as a reference). The latter version of "Cadillac Car" has lost all its edge and relevance, it is disconnected from Black experience, it is not about disempowerment and fantasy anymore, but still it becomes a hit and it obfuscates the original singer (figure 3.5).

Fig. 3.5: Cadillac car, the white version. *Dreamgirls*.

This musical number retells a basic trope from popular music history, illustrated earlier by the Presley version of "Hound Dog": innovation in American music tended to come from Black musicians, but it did not achieve mainstream visibility until it was performed by white artists.

Another number, Jimmy Early's "Fake Your Way to the Top," is both an example of and a comment on the status of Black musicians. Performed in the style of Little Richard, it functions both as advice to the protagonist trio as they start to work under new management, and as a diagnostic on the fate of Black performers in the early 1960s; in the song, Jimmy encourages the young singers to fight disempowerment through glitter and razzle dazzle.

The number also announces some of the film's narrative arc. One can "fake" one's way to the top, achieve fame and fortune, but "reality" can pull one down. Later, the film consistently addresses the pitfalls of Black success. The Dreamettes start doing backup for Early and are then catapulted to success by their manager. It is Taylor who shapes the personae and the sounds of the new trio when they go solo. Along the way, there is a price to be paid: lead singer Effie is pulled to the background for sounding "too real." As discussed, authenticity was central to pop mythologies, but Black "authenticity," or "realness," also implies a cultural identity and in the film the repression of Effie's sound is a sign of how mainstreaming also represses Blackness. Both of the "real" characters in the film, Early and Effie, experience frustration as a result. In the film, Early dies of an overdose after experiencing frustration for not being allowed to develop his art along more socially conscious lines; Effie, on the other hand, leaves the group and struggles as a single mother who's also trying to have a solo career. The crowd-pleasing ending, inherited from the Broadway show, has Effie joining the group one last time before they all start solo careers. The original creator Michael Bennet saw this "positive" ending as problematic: he felt that the logic of the show, as with the logic of history, would have led to the destruction of Effie as it did with Florence Ballard.[26] In the clash between show business mythologies and the frustrations of life, he ultimately chose the former. In Condon's film, this moment has more of an impact thanks to the introduction of a new song for Beyoncé, "Listen," placed shortly before the finale, which both emphasizes her independence and sets the conditions for her reconciliation with Effie.[27] The song brings up the theme of solidarity which the original seemed to lose sight of.[28]

This is all supported by musical styles that range from classic rock to different strands of R & B and soul. In a perfect example of musical narrative integration, one can follow the plot's throughlines by listening to the film's soundtrack. The songs still work independently as decent mock-ups of original hits, and with some important exceptions they do not make literal references to characters or plot events. The early musical numbers at the Detroit theatre, as sung by the Stepp Sisters and Jimmy Early, are references to songs by R & B singers, and the competition winner Little Joe Dixon recalls rock and roll pioneer Fats Domino. Jimmy's theme "Fake Your Way to the Top," referenced earlier, is both a believable R & B song and a way to establish the film's theme of show business success. Together, they establish a mood and a stylistic soundscape, and there are hints of characterization in the Stepp Sisters' "I'm Looking For Something" and the Dreamettes' ironic cry for independence, "Move Out of My Life," a project which the ensuing narrative will challenge. Further along the line, "Cadillac Car" introduces a fantasy of Black belonging, and also that of crossing over into the mainstream. "Dreamgirls," the film's theme song, is, of course, performed on the Copacabana stage as the signature number for the Dreams. The famous intro bears the mark of mainstreaming, and there's very little in the way of Black sound. For narrative purposes it is performed to comment on the trio's mainstream debut, and it focuses the narrative's theme of aspiration, but also of fantasy. This aspiration is fulfilled as the plot progresses; the fantasy is brought down to earth. As with all the other songs in the film, it works both as a character statement and to evoke aspects of narrative context (by bringing to mind the Motown sound), and therefore works both as a comment on the present and a throwback to the past. This number has all the glitter of a generic Motown song, but by engaging with the film's key themes the number acquires emotional force, particularly as the "dream" clashes with reality.

"And I Am Telling You I'm Not Going," the act one curtain song in the original stage show, is one of the key vehicles for musical narration. It was originally conceived as an aria: a showcase number for Jennifer Holliday (figure 3.6). A great deal of the publicity of the film turned around newcomer Jennifer Hudson, who even eclipsed the nominal diva Beyoncé

Fig. 3.6: You're gonna love her. *Dreamgirls*.

and won the Academy Award for her pyrotechnic display of raw emotion in her version. Again, the number works on several levels. Narratively it is a declaration of dependence, a cri de coeur from a strong woman in love. It also signifies her originality and independence: Effie's singing has been considered "too Black" for the Dreams, but here it also comes across as exciting and spectacular, a metonymic vindication of Black talent. Historically, the song is an outburst: it somehow brings back to the film the repressed force of Black styles which would return later as soul. In terms of performance, it also characterizes Effie as a singer along the lines of Aretha Franklin: the "authentic" voice which is a response to the more tamed, mainstream ones of Ross and other Motown singers. Within the diegesis, this moment happens around 1967, one of the years of the Detroit riots, which appear briefly on TV monitors, and this placement contributes to the hints of a political discourse attempted later by Jimmy.

The changes attending the transition of *Dreamgirls* from stage to screen are a sign of an increasing awareness of the need to deal with some of the less visible compromises demanded by racism. But they also point to uses of the history of pop music that bring up new elements of plot. The inclusion of the styles and personalities of that time makes historical struggle clearer by encouraging a different reading of the stars' careers. Finally, the approach to the relationship between the musical numbers and the plot means the songs could maintain their potential for transporting audiences to the past while still providing excitement and glamour.

What Was That? Velvet Goldmine *and the Legacies of Pop*

We have seen fans cheering in Elvis Presley's *Loving You*, swooning in *Bye Bye Birdie* and, of course, emoting hysterically in *A Hard Day's Night* where we witness a real audience acting up like movie characters. Later, fans would feature in non-musical (but musically themed) films such as *This Is Spinal Tap* and *Almost Famous* (2000). Fans in film often appear as irrational, obsessive, noisy, needy, and sometimes, as Chad Bennett suggests in a 2010 article, somewhat embarrassing.[29] They are also, as Bennett proposes in his analysis, invested in popular culture. Fandom is a phenomenon which suggests that music, cinema, and theatre are more than simple artifacts to be appreciated in a detached way by discerning audiences. Fans always read their idols *excessively* (i.e., beyond their literal images and achievements), and this excess is central to the way we have addressed the impact of pop music in narrative film throughout this book. The music fan became a subject in the earliest mythologies of pop music, taking over where movie and theatre fandom had left off, pushing fandom's relevance to culture to new heights. In most instances, fans unproblematically represent the excitement and emotion of the musical performance. The issues raised by the relationship between an audience and music, between personal experience, aesthetics, and marketing, are at the heart of *Velvet Goldmine* where they are revealed as anything but unproblematic. Of the film's pivotal character Arthur (Christian Bale), a journalist and ex-fan with a mission to look into what became of 1970s pop idol Brian Slade, Haynes says:

> He is there for us as a reminder of our place in the cycle of pop and consumer culture, that we're really central to it . . . There's something palpable about intercutting the public sexuality of the rock stars with the very private, unknown sexuality of the consumer, and how one directly affects the other.[30]

Several threads for discussion are suggested by this quote: about the film's structure, about the centrality of sexuality to pop music, but also about Haynes's approach to the power of popular music over an audience. The dynamics between the production of popular culture and its consumers can be explained in different ways. As Stephen N. doCarmo proposes, in articulating a narrative about the tension between the fan and the pop idol, Haynes is acknowledging two disparate versions of the relationship between popular art and its audience.[31] On the one hand, there is the Adorno thesis that popular art creates lies which alienate its audience, making them conform to a hegemonic social order. Certainly, in the film, pop music appears as a lie, driven by financial gain and, in a narrative sleight of hand at the denouement, the lie actually becomes a capitalist truth when the transgressive idol re-emerges in a new role as a stadium rocker supporting a conservative political leader. But on the other hand, as we shall see, Haynes's vision becomes more complex: Firstly, by presenting events as experienced by an individual and remembered a decade later; and, secondly, by placing audiences at the center of the meaning of pop performance. In using the resources of the pop past, as well as adopting a certain perspective about the mythologies pop performances generated, *Velvet Goldmine* becomes an excellent example of a self-referential musical that pushes through the limitations of classic examples of the subgenre.

As in *Dreamgirls*, *Velvet Goldmine* develops its agenda by zeroing in on one particular episode of pop music history to build a wider net of implications: in this case, it is the explosion, and demise, of glam rock in the early seventies and what it meant, in terms of certain fantasies of the self, to young urban kids. Dreaming is important to the meaning of both films: the Black girls' fantasy of reaching mainstream stardom finds echoes in both Brian Slade's storyline (Jonathan Rhys Meyers) and in the story of Arthur's erotic fantasies about his idols (his own narrative is intercut with the official history of Slade and the stories provided by his interviewees). I already addressed the effectiveness of some elements of glam rock in my discussion of *The Rocky Horror Picture Show*. Here, they remain important in proposing a kind of performance that is an invitation: in some sense, *Velvet Goldmine*'s Arthur is the needy, compliant addressee of Frank's "Don't Dream It, Be It." He fails to fulfil the project implicit in the song.

The obvious inspiration for Slade is David Bowie, one of the key personalities in the history of pop. He has an ambivalent status here. One word often used in assessments of the Bowie image is "chameleonic" and the plot pushes this notion to the limit. In the film, such an ability to change might be read as cynical: against the "authenticity" proclaimed by rock, Bowie's persona was obviously fluid, and some would say opportunistic.[32]

Although Bowie did not allow his music to be used in *Velvet Goldmine*, the film is clearly rooted in the period by using themes originally composed by Iggy Pop, Brian Eno, and Marc Bolan. The film does not care too much about Slade's motivations, although the character's evolution suggests an artistic downfall as well as an adaptation to new times. What the film is interested in, however, is the impact of a Bowie-like image on a young man who falls under its spell in the early 1970s. As Haynes suggests in the quote above, he could be any of us.

As the film begins with a fairy tale prologue set in 1854, in which a link is suggested between Oscar Wilde (who was born on that date), as an alien foundling, and the key traits of glam. In the title sequence, we see a colorfully-dressed group of kids heading to a concert by glam rocker Brian Slade in London. The year is 1974. As the concert starts, Slade appears to be shot, in reference to the actual 1973 concert in which Bowie killed off his early persona, the alien "Ziggy Stardust." This is later revealed to be a publicity stunt that will cut Slade's career short and precipitate "the death of glam." In the opening sequence, with credits presented in colourful "pop" fonts, the film mobilizes a utopia which is revealed, as the investigation proceeds, to be founded on precarious premises (thus gesturing toward the Adorno thesis on popular art as a "lie"). After the narrative moves forward to 1984, the film depicts an alternative grey, dull future governed by some generic right-wing regime. Arthur, one of the kids we saw previously, has now grown up to become a journalist in New York. He is a sad, forlorn adult who finds life has not lived up to his expectations, even demonstrated by the film's colour palette which goes literally grey in the 1984 sections. In a section reminiscent in tone and mise en scène of the press room sequence in *Citizen Kane* (1941), he is somewhat casually commissioned to write an article on whatever happened to Slade. The cinephile reference is not an empty gesture: *Velvet Goldmine* explores the idea of biography as process: similar to putting together a puzzle made from different voices.

And as in *Citizen Kane*, Arthur proceeds to piece together some testimonies through Slade's first agent Cecil (Michael Feast), his wife Mandy (Toni Collette), and star Curt Wild (Ewan McGregor). All of them, as well as impresario Jerry Devine (Eddie Izzard) have counterparts in real people surrounding Bowie in the early 1970s. Although the parallels are quite literal in the cases of Cecil, Mandy, and Devine, Wild has been the subject of some speculation. As acknowledged by Haynes, he is meant to recall Iggy Pop, who started a short artistic relationship with Bowie in the early 1970s, although Haynes has explained that he took elements from other American rockers of the period, like Lou Reed. It was Reed who, according to legend, suffered electroshock therapy when he was a boy, as Wild does in the film.[33] And Reed had a smoother relationship with Bowie than Iggy Pop had. In the end, what was important for Haynes was the relationship between British and American versions of pop music.[34] More generally, Haynes is taking advantage of a repertoire of mythologies and personalities to develop the way they affect an audience. During Arthur's investigation, Cecil, Mandy, and Wild will tell their part of the story, but nobody says anything which is not already on the public record. It is in the flashbacks that the musical numbers take place, and they are mostly performed by Slade. We see his beginnings in a small club; his hesitations about finding a style, eventually manufactured by a flamboyant manager who packages him to the delight of a boardroom of businessmen; and his ambition for stardom. It is interesting that, just as the Slade persona fascinates Arthur, we see Wild in his first performance through Slade's eyes (or, more precisely, we see Cecil's version of the facts as imagined by Arthur) (figure 3.7). Pop performance is both a spectacle and a life-changing experience. Another musical number has Slade

Fig. 3.7: The idol as fan. *Velvet Goldmine.*

and Wild performing together, and towards the end, the numbers define the excessive, tired image that Slade is acquiring, thus mirroring the character's arc.

Devine lures Slade away from Cecil and turns him into a commercial product, very much as Curtis Taylor does with the Dreams in *Dreamgirls*. Under Devine's management, Slade becomes a superstar by establishing a provocative, spectacular image (the Maxwell Demon persona), which now seems to be, in another echo of the Adorno diagnostic on popular music, at the service of suited businessmen. One musical number represents his new image: artful, campy, and sophisticated, which presents every cliché of queer culture, from the costumes to the homoeroticism, packaged for mass consumption. The film is structured in such a way that its audience is always looking at Slade, but there are no solid clues as to his actual identity: all that we see could be a mask or a pose. As in *Citizen Kane*, we never hear Slade's version of things, even if he is alive during the diegesis (unlike *Citizen Kane*). Slade's always represented as a construct created by Devine, by the imaginations of Cecil or Mandy, or by Arthur's fantasies. Slade starts off flirting with folk and flower power but is later inspired by Little Richard (we see him "faking" Richard as a child) and glam rock pioneer Jack Fairy. Fairy is not based on any particular figure, but he evokes the spirit of Richard in one central aspect according to Haynes: "In a strange way, Fairy is meant to be the Little Richard of glam rock . . . I think he's there to contrast the consumerist drive to the famous, which often is more effective with the very driven, self-conscious stealer of ideas than it is with the organic originator of the same ideas."[35] Pop music, then, is not just about commerce or the elicitation of enthusiasm from fans: it carries ideas, it engages with politics and identities. More specifically, in the film's mythology, Fairy is the inheritor of the queer identity that goes back to Oscar Wilde, a heritage represented as a green, pinned carnation that travels from one generation to the next and that means resistance, identity, and survival. Slade steals the symbolic carnation from Fairy: his possession of it may be illegitimate, but what matters is how a certain spirit is communicated in spite of such illegitimacy. Even if his version of glam rock is commercial and maybe cynical, the original elements remain and are passed on to Arthur (by Curt) in the narrative.

Slade gets Devine to also sign up Wild, who is going through a rough patch due to drug addiction: for Slade, the collaboration is cemented by the fascination he feels for Wild's "realness" (in a knowing nod to the frustrated collaboration between Bowie and Iggy Pop); for the manager, the match is another business opportunity (we see cartoonish "dollar signs" in his eyes as he contemplates the partnership). The trope of selling out, the opposition between the authentic and the fake, and the "bad" manager, are all motifs from the mythologies of pop.[36] Slade is portrayed as something of a betrayer. He absorbs energies from queer showbusiness (the drag traditions represented by his uncle, Little Richard, Jack Fairy, and even Curt Wild) but fails to make them completely his. *Velvet Goldmine* treats sexuality with a certain ambivalence, which the film refuses to resolve completely. Neither Slade nor Wild are explicitly presented as "gay," although the film presents some deep mutual bond, and on a couple of occasions it is hinted that "things" may have happened (certainly homosexual sex being among them). The ambivalence is further compounded by Wild's response to a reporter near the start of the film, which in a way sounds more like Haynes's authorial voice than the character's own:

> Everyone's into this scene because it's supposedly the thing to do right now. But you just can't fake being gay. If they claim they're gay they're going to have to make love in gay style, and most of these kids . . . they just won't be able to make it. That line, "Everybody's bisexual," that's a very popular thing to say right now. I think it's meaningless.[37]

This sounds like a denial of sexual nonconformity, as it suggests it might just be an attempt to be cool; on the other hand, elsewhere we see the queerer elements of Slade's identity (as a teenager we see him about to have sex with a much younger kid in exchange for a gold watch), which suggest that if his "homosexuality" was not completely "authentic" it was neither completely "fake."[38] Resistance to "gay" identity was as much a trademark of glam rock as claims of general, polysexual desire. So in a way, the Slade-Wild plotline within *Velvet Goldmine* is at least hinting that even sexualities and desires may have been part of an act, the kind of fakery pop stars pull all the time to keep an audience interested. The facts do not matter as much as the impression they create, and as we shall see they do create a strong impression on teen Arthur.

Citizen Kane does not concern itself too much with its journalist, Thompson, who is always kept in the shadows, asking questions but without an individual backstory. In contrast, Arthur's character arc becomes the main plot of the film: he turns out to be the film's fourth perspective on Slade (following Cecil, Mandy, and Curt) and the story's flesh-and-blood Rosebud. Even more importantly, his experience is inserted into the structure of the film to become the dominant point of view. The memories of Cecil and Mandy seem to rekindle Arthur's own memories of being fascinated by Slade (figure 3.8): every event in Slade's story seems to have its counterpart in the process of Arthur becoming what he is. We learn, through flashbacks, some key points in his evolution: he was a shy teenager, ashamed of his own desire (figure 3.9), who then leaves home in search of the freedom of the city. Although the 1984 version of Arthur does not convey joy, his life as an adult still leads him to recall a moment of glory. While trying to get some insights from Wild, whom he encounters almost casually, he remembers how, after a concert to celebrate the end of glam rock, he shared an erotic moment with him, presented in a glowing flashback. The film's logic does not lead one to believe this moment has a significant impact on Arthur's life, but symbolically it is charged: after they have sex, both of them look at the starry sky where a spaceship, in reference to both the "alien" Ziggy and the "alien" Oscar Wilde as

Fig. 3.8: The fan's fascination. *Velvet Goldmine.*

Fig. 3.9: The fan's shame. *Velvet Goldmine.*

introduced at the film's start, is glimpsed bringing some glitter into their world.

No matter that popular culture is entangled with opportunism, commercialism, and exploitation, it has a very real impact on its audience in helping them shape their worldviews and identities. Songs, like movies, articulate a broad range of emotions. As for Arthur, specifically, his brush with glam rock as a teenager remains one identity-making event, that cannot be erased. Through the mystique of pop, Arthur becomes what he is, and discovering some hidden truth about his idol is not going to change things much. At the start, as he rushes towards Slade's fateful concert, he briefly brushes past Jack Fairy. It is a detail which will be developed in the story: Slade may have stolen the flame of camp survival from Fairy, but it will eventually end up in Arthur's power. In short, Arthur is a gay everyman, his story is the story of many gay men in the seventies, unsure, ashamed, bullied. Popular culture, in particular music, is part of his personal and political liberation. Bennett summarizes this as follows:

> *Velvet Goldmine* mourns the loss of the rich excess of affect surrounding Arthur's adolescence and the glam era: the teenage Arthur scampers through the adult Arthur's memory and the movie wearing a perpetual, heartbreaking blush, and the film parallels

Slade's ascent to stardom with Arthur's memories of "all the things" of this lost youth at odds with normative culture, especially his now repressed fandom and queer sexuality.[39]

In accounting for the particular links between glam rock musical performance and its consumers, we are very close to Dyer's considerations on disco: granted, as with every popular form, it is the result of capitalism, but it can also contribute to strengthen cultural identities and to forge community links.[40] In both cases, popular music brings about personal liberation. Although Dyer acknowledges the "capitalist" basis for popular music, he insists it also unlocks areas of human experience that need to be produced outside of the mainstream. And of course, as Bennett suggests, such processes of appropriation through misreading are particularly important for a queer audience. Fans have, of course, always been a part of musicals, and show business mythologies have had an impact on them. A frequent arc for the fan character of movies and stage shows is to become a star themselves. But as long as the pop musical engages with the production of popular song in more complex ways (that is, rather than concealing its process), and as long as it continues to expand its repertoire of addressees, it can provide a deeper version of the fan as consumer.

In the end, *Velvet Goldmine* mistrusts the utopian elements of pop music's promise: not only is it revealed as a lie, but it also does not bring any permanent joy. Yet, it presents popular music as a vehicle to establish a link with the past which, at least, opens up areas of previously underexplored experience. The meaning behind the narrative in some ways recalls the verdict of *Dreamgirls*: pop stardom is often based on lies, may be achieved through illegal means, and it is often unfair to the people who get left behind, but pop stars also have a considerable impact on ordinary lives. Aligning with Dyer's reflection, Haynes's focus is on issues of sexuality and identity, two areas that any discussion of pop music always orbit around. In some limited way, and for a specific audience, pop music did achieve something like a utopia.

CONCLUSION

Qualified Joys

This book set out to investigate the impact of pop music, the dominant type of popular music since the late 1950s, on the Hollywood musical, and to characterize the result of that influence as a new species, the pop musical. Continuities have been identified that justify the pop musical as the outcome of a line of evolution within the Hollywood musical which can be characterized variously by: the tension between integration and attractions; the use of the past to reach audiences through nostalgia; and through the consolidation of certain sub-genres such as the biopic or the dance musical. Despite this, the three types identified by Altman—the show musical, the fairy tale musical and the folk musical—all remain central to the new canon, demonstrating the persistence and consistency of the genre at large. But there are also discontinuities, developments, and transformations caused by the end of the classical genre system, as well as by traits which are specific to the post-1955 manifestations of popular music, including (but not limited to) rock, soul, doo wop, glam rock, disco, and rap: these styles inflect such continuities and in their own specific ways produce innovation. Like other film genres, the Hollywood musical has become less pure, and so examples that seem far from the genre as classical fans have understood it, like *Saturday Night Fever*, need to be considered also as part of the genre's updated tradition. This evolution has certainly affected other classical film genres in similar ways. Narrative and aesthetic conventions and thematic repertoires have become more flexible, each genre has become less fixed and there have emerged formal explorations that classical frameworks previously discouraged. The drive towards a more realistic approach to representation (one that shows awareness of the complexity of the world), a salient feature of the move from classical to post-classical manifestations, has been particularly disruptive to the tradition of the classical musical, since musicals have tended to be essentially anti-realist and have featured reassuring agendas that confirmed fixed mythologies about gender and race. Forms of pop music like rap or soul carry with them elements of their relationship with social realities, and their appearance in musicals like *Beat Street* or *Dreamgirls* have strengthened their connections to a historical moment and specific communities. Even if such a drive towards realism is common to all genres (westerns, war films, even romantic comedies become more realistic in the post-classical era), my main concern here has been to discuss changes that specifically affect the musical.

As outlined in the introduction, the move towards the pop musical form was initiated when two different dynamics, those of the continually evolving record industry and those of post-classical Hollywood, started to seek some sort of accommodation between them, almost as soon as rock and roll became an undeniable force in capturing its audience's attention in the mid-1950s. One basic obstacle for that accommodation was the non-dramatic substance of the pop song. It was important to develop ways to communicate narrative context, the story itself, and characterization in pop songs. The Broadway musical, particularly since the 1940s, had been experimenting with bringing musical elements (composition, lyrics, dance) and dramatic elements closer together (which is one way of explaining "integration"), and some examples suggest that the stage musical continues to be a source of inspiration for the new musical—just as it was in the classical period. While the earliest demonstrations of pop music's potential within the Hollywood musical can be found in jukebox musicals of the mid- to late-1950s, it is in a Broadway adaptation, *Bye Bye Birdie*, that we find a couple of "rock" numbers which have a dramatic place in the narrative and glimpses of understanding for how the new musical styles might work within a story. Rock and roll music is here associated with the younger protagonists and it makes a contribution to characterization and plot. A decade later, the earliest musicals using pop songs to tell a story (*Jesus Christ Superstar, Tommy, Godspell* (1973), *The*

Rocky Horror Picture Show) were all seen first in (non-mainstream) stage versions. It is at this point, in the early seventies, when objections against rock's dramatic potential start to disappear and it becomes increasingly clear that pop music and storytelling can work together in ways that go beyond mere juxtaposition.

But if stage traditions contribute to strengthening the relationship between narrative and a pop score, the semantic elements in the pop musical borrow more substantially from a repertoire of ideas and mythologies which emerges out of the 1960s pop song. As pop music became more sophisticated and achieved historical and social prominence, it also acquired the potential to influence elements of the pop musical, making it effectively a two-way relationship. Many instances in this book show how pop music affected not just the content of the new musicals but created new possibilities at other textual levels. The inflections we have addressed in this essay happened on four basic levels: industrial, formal, social, and ideological.

Industrially, Hollywood had to open itself up to the dynamics of record companies. Developing synergies was important, as these were originally two separate businesses. The difficulties in bridging the gap between them, as outlined in chapter two, account for the tensions we have seen, particularly during the sixties. We saw, for instance, how Elvis Presley, the first rock megastar, was forced to choose between growing up as a pop star or as a Hollywood star, as if those pathways were incompatible, and we saw that investment in youth pop musicals was more likely at lower-stakes companies like AIP, whereas big studios continued investing in old-fashioned stage adaptations such as *My Fair Lady*, *The Sound of Music*, *Funny Girl*, and *Hello Dolly* (1969). But by the late 1960s, music men, like Robert Stigwood and, later, Berry Gordy, were finding ways to develop opportunities in the pop musical through marketing and star presence. It is Stigwood who finds, through his work on *Saturday Night Fever*, a successful formula, which was also later explored by his co-producer Allan Carr, and that later still will give rise to a number of musicals produced with the support of record companies and starring pop singers.

Formally, the pop musical feels different from the classical musical because pop songs were conceived independently from a dramatic context (unlike a large portion of American pop music in the twentieth century, which originated in different types of stage shows). Again, its beginnings were difficult since early pop songs were essentially unambitious in dramatic terms. No analysis can make songs like Paul Anka's "Diana," the Supremes' "Baby Love," The Beach Boys' "California Girls," or even Bill Haley's "Rock Around the Clock" lyrically sophisticated or filled with ideas or narrative content. Contemporary pop songs have been dismissed as generic and undramatic. Still, their impact cannot be denied: they work on levels that reach beyond formal attributes. It is that impact that the pop musical can explore. Each pop song has the potential to bring up substantial slices of personal or collective experience. Pop songs are memory capsules that evoke past experiences. Most importantly, as discussed in chapter 3, the music developed and diversified. Pop is not a monolithic category and it evolved and developed a very broad lexicon throughout the late 1960s and onwards. What the examples studied suggest is that rather than containing lyrics with a literal meaning that propel the action, the pop musical tends to use other semantic layers of the song: the period they evoke, their ideology, their relationship with specific demographics. Songs—as in *Dirty Dancing*, *Beat Street*, and *Moulin Rouge!*—may not be so specifically tied to the demands of plot and character, but they still contribute to the film's overall meaning by evoking a time or a mood. In this sense, pop can work as a repertoire with differently inflected styles that can be absorbed into the musical film. Glam rock, for example, carries connotations that can be developed in films as different as *The Rocky Horror Picture Show* and *Velvet Goldmine*.

Socially speaking, pop music started simply as youth music—something designed to reach that certain demographic—and as the 1960s progressed it then engaged deeply with changes in American society that had to do with politics, ideology, race, and sexuality. Both its youth-friendly qualities and its dialogue with the social invigorated the genre in ways that would have been impossible with pre-1955 styles. Beyond demographics, pop music developed a new relationship with its listeners. Traditional popular music was seldom rebellious or anti-conventional. The new pop music was at first resisted by the establishment as an affront to morality, and thereafter it retained these new mythologies, that the musical could now borrow from. From the very start, the pop musical's relationship with its young audience meant a very specific world had to be represented, an excellent example of this being the sun-kissed youth utopia of the API beach party cycle. So the new pop music was an ideal vehicle to bring themes of social conflict, race, and sex into the musical. Given the dominance of the new pop music, it also became a signifier of lived experience. The pop musical can deal with a broader range of identities than the more explicitly conservative classical musical. In this book we have seen how the connotations of pop intensify discourses on sexuality in *Velvet Goldmine* and on race in *Dreamgirls*. For a very substantial majority of a contemporary audience, the traditions of pop are their only experience of popular music.

Finally, in ideological terms, three of the key mythologies that gave the genre coherence in its classical age are centrally challenged in the pop musical. The first one had to do with its utopian potentialities: the utopian impulse of the musical is now faced with the intriguing question, formulated by Richard Dyer, that implies that utopia has winners and losers, "Utopia for whom?" The pop musical necessarily addresses utopia as partial, and even precarious (which doesn't necessarily mean that it does away with it altogether). The second myth is the mystique of the heterosexual couple. The pop musical retains a lot of this mystique about love, which shows continuity with one of the most important semantic elements of the genre, but now it does not need to be central, sacred, uncomplicated, or heterosexual. And it often does not last forever. Even when mystified (as in *Moulin Rouge!*) it can end badly. In *Rocketman*, *The Rocky Horror Picture Show*, and *Velvet Goldmine*, heterosexual couplings and even the mystique of love, are rendered as deceitful and secondary to the film's overall project. And thirdly, the myth of show business, which was presented as having some kind of magical healing power in traditional musicals (acting in synchronicity with heterosexual love) is also revealed as corrupt, problematic, commercial, and quite capable of causing suffering, as evidenced in *Dreamgirls* and *Velvet Goldmine*. Show business is rarely wholeheartedly celebrated at the end of pop musicals.

These new inflections will in turn have an impact on the original mythologies underlying Altman's three musical types. The fairy tale musical initially proposed enchanted kingdoms, apt for the genre's utopian drive: it reinforced certain notions of arcadia and offered images of paradise. In the non-traditional pop musical however, death lurks everywhere (*Moulin Rouge!* is, once again, a good example, as is *Little Shop of Horrors*), but even when it doesn't, these fairy tale worlds are more complex, more dangerous than in the past. Disappointment, illness, and corruption threaten these enchanted kingdoms and sometimes they can become nightmarish forests where painful decisions must be made, and character opposites are not always brought together through love as they used to be. Utopias are now tarnished. The backstage musical presented a metaphor of society through show business. Crucially, this musical type concealed the work involved for the creation of a stage show. Show business had magical powers: it could be produced through simple enthusiasm and spontaneity. The American show business mythology presents an ideal society where everybody has their place, where heterosexual love always triumphs, where talent and a spirit of community can get anything done. Now, with the pop musical version, all the internal workings of show business are on display and the stakes are higher: the final diegetic performances in *Beat Street* and *Dreamgirls* come about after suffering and compromise. Pain is not concealed; endings are not always happy. The pop musical is not afraid to represent its characters sweating for their art. Finally, the folk musical originally created a harmonious version of community that the later pop musical did not always reinforce. In any case, communities are acknowledged as fragmented, and never perfect. Some of my examples, such as *Saturday Night Fever* or *Velvet Goldmine*, even end by finding their communities lacking, so that characters leave them behind, creating in the process pain and tears.

Classical film genres all suffered transformations in the post-classical period. Some were close to extinction. It is tempting to propose the idea of the death of classical genres, but certainly the musical was not as dead as some have argued. The pop musical may not do everything as successfully as classical musicals did, at least when considered by a particular audience. But it does capture imaginations. Pop music's history, its moods, and its memories, has had a resurgence in the twenty-first century, as evidenced by: the TV pop musical, musical documentaries, sophisticated music videos, filmed concerts, and a few movie musicals. These all suggest that the rumors of its death were greatly exaggerated.

NOTES

Introduction: The Hollywood Musical Is Dead. Long Live the Hollywood Musical!

1. For a sustained discussion of new elements introduced in the 1966–1983 period, see Kelly Kessler, *Destabilizing the Hollywood Musical: Music, Masculinity and Mayhem* (Basingstoke, UK: Palgrave Macmillan, 2010).
2. Stanley Green's *The Encyclopaedia of Musical Film* (New York: Oxford University Press, 1981) did not even include Elvis Presley, and Clive Hirschhorn keeps "Rock Musicals" in a separate section after attempting the most complete overview of the genre until 1981.
3. Barry, Keith Grant, *The Hollywood Film Musical* (Chichester, UK: John Wiley & Sons, 2012).
4. Desirée J. Garcia, *The Migration of Musical Film: From Ethnic Margins to American Mainstream* (New Brunswick, N.J.: Rutgers University Press, 2014).
5. Kessler, *Destabilizing the Hollywood Musical.*
6. Sean Griffin, *Free and Easy? A Defining History of the American Film Musical Genre* (Oxford: John Wiley & Sons, 2017).
7. Dave Kehr, "Can't Stop the Musicals," *American Film* 9, no. 7 (1984): 35–36.
8. Two thirds of the total number of musicals were made between 1927 and 1947, with only one third produced in the following forty years. Rick Altman, *The American Film Musical* (Bloomington: Indiana University Press, 1987), 198.
9. YouTube channel *Sideways* explores some of the issues created by recent pop musical culture vs. traditional integrated musical narration in a series of videos on post-1987 Disney musicals. The 2019 video "The Problem with *Tarzan*" specifically highlights the difference between music videos and integrated songs.

Sideways, "The Problem with Tarzan," YouTube video, 20:39, July 31, 2019, https://youtu.be/rMJ8FyQiM4Y.

10. Similar dismissals of pop music as material for musicals can be found in Mark N. Grant, *The Rise and Fall of the Broadway Musical* (Hanover, N.H.: University Press of New England, 2004) and in Ethan Mordden, *Open a New Window: The Broadway Musical in the 1960s* (New York: St. Martin's Press, 2015).

11. Donald Clarke, *The Rise and Fall of Popular Music* (London: Viking, 1995).

12. See Tim Wall, *Studying Popular Music Culture*, 2nd ed. (London: Sage, 2013), 173–174.

13. See Elijah Wald, *How the Beatles Destroyed Rock 'n' Roll: An Alternative History of American Popular Music* (New York: Oxford University Press, 2009), 212.

14. Richard A. Peterson, "Why 1955? Explaining the Advent of Rock Music," *Popular Music* 9, no. 1 (1990): 97–116.

15. Glenn C. Altschuler, *All Shook Up: How Rock 'n' Roll Changed America* (New York: Oxford University Press, 2003), 35–65.

16. The approach to pop music and the way it impacted the movies in this book is indebted to work by Simon Frith, Lawrence Grossberg, Dick Hebdige, Richard Dyer, and Tony Bennett, who establish strong links between society, consumption, and the "uses" of different strands of pop music. It is my premise that a shift in the former will affect the way movies deal with the latter.

17. Simon Frith, *Music for Pleasure: Essays in the Sociology of Pop* (New York: Routledge, 1988).

18. Iain Chambers, *Urban Rhythms: Pop Music and Popular Culture* (London: MacMillan, 1985), 7.

19. Pierre Bourdieu, *Distinction: A Social Critique of the Judgement of Taste* (Cambridge, Mass.: Harvard University Press, 1984).

20. Dick Hebdige, "Subculture: The Meaning of Style," *Critical Quarterly* 37, no. 2 (1995): 120–124.

21. See Altschuler, *All Shook Up*, 3–34. In this first chapter, he chronicles the aversion to early rock in the media from politicians and religious institutions.

22. Not coincidentally for our purposes, 1955 marked the release of Nicholas Ray's *Rebel Without a Cause*, one key instance that shows the "problematic" teenager as a source of concern for adults.

23. Simon Reynolds, *Shock and Awe: Glam Rock and Its Legacy, from the Seventies to the Twenty-First Century* (London: Faber & Faber, 2016) explores the recycling of pop music traditions.

24. Marshall Crenshaw, *Hollywood Rock: A Guide to Rock 'n' Roll in the Movies* (New York: Harper Perennial, 1994).

25. Frith, *Music for Pleasure*, 1.

26. Even if "rock" has been reworked beyond recognition, and superseded numerous times since 1955, the concept has acquired cultural centrality and it has kept mythic resonance—only really challenged by the emergence of hip-hop culture in the 1970s. It is the idea of rock, rather than actual rock and roll music, that justifies its importance throughout this book as a structuring concept.

27. For a slightly different diagnostic to the one presented here, see Frith, *Music for Pleasure*, 1. According to him, the rock era was "born around 1956 with Elvis Presley, peaking around 1967 with *Sgt. Pepper*, dying around 1976 with the Sex Pistols."

28. Lawrence Grossberg, "The Framing of Rock: Rock and the New Conservatism," in *Rock and Popular Music: Policies, Politics, Institutions*, ed. Tony Bennett, Simon Frith, Lawrence Grossberg, John Shepherd, and Graeme Turner (London: Routledge, 2005), 207.

29. Bob Stanley, *Yeah Yeah Yeah: The Story of Modern Pop* (London: Faber & Faber, 2013), xiii.

30. Richard Dyer, "In Defense of Disco," *New Formations* 58, no. 58 (1979): 101–108.

31. For a social history of the strands making up "pop music," see Paul Friedlander, *Rock and Roll: A Social History* (Boulder, Colo.: Westview Press, 1996).

32. Sean Griffin, *Free and Easy? A Defining History of the American Film Musical Genre* (Oxford: John Wiley & Sons, 2017).

33. In his introduction, Griffin explains how he kept on testing certain films against the category "Hollywood Musical" and how his respondents were sometimes reluctant, sometimes hostile to the application of the label to films such as *Saturday Night Fever* or *Dirty Dancing*. Griffin, *Free and Easy?*, 2.

34. See Jane Feuer, "Is Dirty Dancing a Musical, and Why Should It Matter?," in *The Time of Our Lives: Dirty Dancing and Popular Culture*, ed. Yannis Tzioumakis and Siân Lincoln (Detroit: Wayne State University Press, 2013); and Richard Dyer, *In the Space of a Song: The Uses of Song in Film* (London: Routledge, 2012).

35. K. J. Donnelly and Beth Carroll, eds., *Contemporary Musical Film* (Edinburgh: Edinburgh University Press, 2017).

36. A test case could be *American Graffiti* (1973). It does fulfill most of the conditions put forward: the film's agenda would not work (i.e., the film would not hold the same meaning) without the song soundtrack. Still, it is not a very good example of the issues of the pop musical: some of the songs in *American Graffiti* seem to refer to the story at various points, but most don't. There is no sustained dancing to the music, and characters don't react to the lyrics. The soundtrack is merely a running commentary that says more about the general mood than about the characters and plot developments.

37. Garcia, *The Migration of Musical Film*.

38. Jane Feuer, *The Hollywood Musical* (Basingstoke, UK: Macmillan Press, 1993).

39. Kimberley Monteyne, *Hip Hop on Film: Performance Culture, Urban Space, and Genre Transformation in the 1980s* (Jackson: University Press of Mississippi, 2013).

40. There is some reluctance to consider rap as pop music. The debate is pertinent. However, within the limits of this essay, hip-hop culture is often presented as closer to the dynamics of pop than it is to the particular ideal and representation of "authenticity" in rock.

41. Dyer, *In the Space of a Song*, 31.

42. Jane Feuer, *The Hollywood Musical* (London: MacMillan Education UK, 1993), 26–30.
43. Richard Dyer, "Entertainment and Utopia," in *Only Entertainment* (London: Routledge, 1992), 19–35.
44. This idea is developed in Ray Knapp, *The American Musical and the Formation of National Identity* (Princeton, N.J.: Princeton University Press, 2005).
45. Arthur Knight, *Disintegrating the Musical: Black Performance and American Musical Film* (Durham, N.C.: Duke University Press, 2002).
46. See Matthew Tinkcom, *Working Like a Homosexual: Camp, Capital, Cinema* (Durham, N.C.: Duke University Press, 2002); and Steven Cohan, *Incongruous Entertainment: Camp, Cultural Value, and the MGM Musical* (Durham, N.C.: Duke University Press, 2005).
47. Ryan Bunch, "'Love is an Open Door,'" in *Contemporary Musical Film*, ed. K. J. Donnelly and Beth Carroll (Edinburgh: Edinburgh University Press, 2017), 100.
48. Limitations of space prevent me from discussing the specifics of musical styles. Wall's *Studying Popular Music Culture* provides an introduction to some technical issues. For a more sustained discussion of musicological aspects of pop music, see Theodore Gracyk's *Listening to Popular Music* (Ann Arbor: University of Michigan Press, 2007).
49. See David Baker, "Rock Rebels and Delinquents: The Emergence of the Rock Rebel in 1950s 'Youth Problem' Films," *Journal of Media and Cultural Studies* 19, no. 1 (2005): 39–54.
50. Ian Inglis, "Popular Music History on Screen: The Pop/Rock Biopic," *Popular Music History* 2, no. 1 (2007): 77–93.
51. Dyer, *In the Space of a Song*; Altman, *The American Film Musical*.
52. Inglis, "Popular Music History on Screen," 88–89.
53. Griffin, *Free and Easy?*, 290–292.
54. Marco Calavita, "'MTV Aesthetics' at the Movies: Interrogating a Film Criticism Fallacy," *Journal of Film and Video* 59, no. 3 (2007): 15–31.
55. For a clear discussion on the premises and effects of the "integration" tradition, see Geoffrey Block, *Enchanted Evenings: The Broadway Musical from "Show Boat" to Sondheim and Lloyd Webber* (New York: Oxford University Press, 2009).
56. Joseph Andrew Casper, *Vincente Minnelli and the Film Musical* (New York: AS Barnes, 1977).
57. Scott McMillin, *The Musical as Drama* (Princeton, N.J.: Princeton University Press, 2014).
58. John Mueller, "Fred Astaire and the Integrated Musical," *Cinema Journal* 24, no. 1 (1984): 28–40.
59. In a different way, Nina Penner problematizes the issues I am raising here, by focusing on the opposition between "diegetic" and "non-diegetic" musical numbers. Nina Penner, "Rethinking the Diegetic/Nondiegetic Distinction in the Film Musical," *Music and the Moving Image* 10, no. 3 (2017): 3–20.

1. Hollywood and the Rise of Pop Music: The Age of Elvis

1. For an overview of reactions to Elvis, see Glenn C. Altschuler, *All Shook Up: How Rock 'n' Roll Changed America* (New York: Oxford University Press, 2003), 2–10.
2. Altschuler, *All Shook Up*, 86.
3. See Benson P. Fraser and William J. Brown, "Media, Celebrities, and Social Influence: Identification with Elvis Presley," *Mass Communication and Society* 5, no. 2 (2002): 183–206, for an analysis of fans' continuing identification with the Elvis persona.
4. B. Lee Cooper, "Before Elvis: The Prehistory of Rock 'n' Roll," *Rock Music Studies* 1, no. 1 (2014): 97–99.
5. Elijah Wald, *How the Beatles Destroyed Rock 'n' Roll: An Alternative History of American Popular Music* (New York: Oxford University Press, 2009).
6. See Altschuler, *All Shook Up*, which provides a full account of the social ramifications of the rock 'n' roll phenomenon.
7. Some examples are: *Teen Age Thunder* (1957), *High School Hellcats* (1957), *Juvenile Jungle* (1958), and *Live Fast, Die Young* (1958).
8. Elsewhere, others were less reluctant during this period. Great Britain, for instance, was more open to including pop stars in musicals from the late 1950s, as the cases of Tommy Steele and Cliff Richard attest. The pop musicals starring Richard, in particular, functioned as vehicles for mildly challenging (though still conservative) mythologies about class and sexuality. The pop musical in Britain showed the budding counterculture of cafés, where folk met rock and spearheaded the sexual revolution. As early as 1964, the almost shockingly modern *A Hard Day's Night* was released. More influenced by the European New Wave styles than by the conventions of the Hollywood musical, it was a perfect example of how pop music could contribute to cinematic innovation. While capitalizing on the Beatles phenomenon, and culminating in a TV concert, Richard Lester's film is responding to the very essence of the new pop music just as it exploded in American culture.
9. Cited in Altschuler, *All Shook Up*, 6.
10. See Elizabeth L. Wollman, *The Theater Will Rock: A History of the Rock Musical, from Hair to Hedwig* (Ann Arbor: University of Michigan Press, 2006), 18: "'Honestly Sincere' borrows from rock 'n' roll in other respects, it is scored for electric guitar, bass, drums and brass section, it features a syncopated walking bass line; and the melody is built largely of short, repeated melodic fragments in a narrow range."
11. For the movie version, Albert became a chemistry teacher. Clearly English did not sound as cool.
12. Interestingly, a role played originally by Latino performer Chita Rivera was de-Latinized for the Hollywood version where it was played by Leigh wearing a black wig.
13. Wollman, *The Theater Will Rock*.

14. Wollman, *The Theater Will Rock*, 19.
15. Wollman engages with less significant attempts in the late 1950s and 1960s, but she acknowledges that neither Broadway critics nor audiences were generally in favor of hearing rock scores on stage before *Hair*.
16. See Altschuler, *All Shook Up*; David E. James, *Rock 'n 'Film: Cinema's Dance with Popular Music* (New York: Oxford University Press, 2015).
17. This first wave would lose momentum by 1958, but by then its impact was indelible and provided the starting point for a series of trends that were not exactly rock and roll but would not have existed without it.
18. Historians of the rise of pop music devote some attention to companies making secret payments to radio stations in exchange for airplay. This scandal erupted into the public sphere in 1960, which seriously affected the industry. For an extended account, see R. H. Coase, "Payola in Radio and Television Broadcasting," *Journal of Law & Economics* 22, no. 2 (1979): 269–328. The payola scandals are referenced in the "Stepping to the Bad Side" number in *Dreamgirls*.
19. Altschuler, *All Shook Up*, 55.
20. Julie Lobalzo Wright articulates this change by using the expression "the taming of Elvis Presley." See Julie Lobalzo Wright, *Crossover Stardom: Popular Male Music Stars in American Cinema* (New York: Bloomsbury Publishing USA, 2017), 53.
21. David E. James highlights the lack of Black presence in Elvis's later 1960s films. See James, *Rock 'n' Film*, 103–106.
22. James, *Rock 'n' Film*, 83.
23. The "double love interest" is also featured in *King Creole*, with Dolores Hart again playing the "good innocent" girlfriend, set against the more mature, compromised woman played by Carolyn Jones.
24. See Greil Marcus, *Mystery Train: Images of America in Rock 'n' Roll Music* (New York: Penguin, 2015), 338.
25. See his morphology of the Elvis film in James, *Rock 'n' Film*, 100–101.
26. Joy T. Taylor, "'You Can't Spend Your Whole Life on a Surfboard': Elvis Presley, Exotic Whiteness, and Native Performance in *Blue Hawaii* and *Girls! Girls! Girls!*," *Quarterly Review of Film and Video* 32, no. 1 (2015): 21–37.
27. James doesn't mention them in his comprehensive *Rock 'n' Film*.
28. Gary Morris, "Beyond the Beach: Social and Formal Aspects of AIP's Beach Party Movies," *Journal of Popular Film and Television* 21, no. 1 (1993): 7.
29. Morris, "Beyond the Beach," for some examples of the different connotations the beach had in earlier films.
30. Morris, "Beyond the Beach," 9.
31. For an extended discussion of late Elvis films, see Lobalzo Wright, *Crossover Stardom*, 71.
32. R. L. Rutsky, "Surfing the Other: Ideology on the Beach," *Film Quarterly* 52, no. 4 (1999): 15.
33. "I Think, You Think," is a song from *Beach Blanket Bingo* that allows the characters to banter with each other. It can be considered part of a tradition that

includes the Astaire and Rogers number, "Let's Call the Whole Thing Off," from *Shall We Dance?* (1937).

34. Morris, "Beyond the Beach."

35. Rutsky, "Surfing the Other," 13.

36. Examples discussed later include *Saturday Night Fever, Little Shop of Horrors, Dreamgirls,* and *Velvet Goldmine,* all of which set up and then undermine their utopian spaces.

2. Embracing Pop: Integrating the Pop Musical

1. See Elizabeth L. Wollman, *The Theater Will Rock: A History of the Rock Musical, from Hair to Hedwig* (Ann Arbor: University of Michigan Press, 2006), esp. 41–64, and Scott Warfield, "From Hair to Rent: Is 'Rock' a Four-Letter Word on Broadway?," in *The Cambridge Companion to the Musical,* ed. William A. Everett and Paul R. Laird (Cambridge: Cambridge University Press, 2002), 231–245.

2. Ethan Mordden, *Open a New Window: The Broadway Musical in the 1960s* (New York: St. Martin's Press, 2015), 231.

3. For an example of this perspective, see Donald Clarke, *The Rise and Fall of Popular Music* (London: Viking, 1995).

4. See Mark N. Grant, *The Rise and Fall of the Broadway Musical* (Hanover, N.H.: University Press of New England, 2004), 150–165, and Warfield, "From Hair to Rent." Elizabeth L. Wollman, in her book on rock in the Broadway musical provides examples of musical performers who care less about intelligibility when they sing in a rock idiom. See Wollman, *The Theater Will Rock,* 202.

5. Elijah Wald, *How the Beatles Destroyed Rock 'n' Roll: An Alternative History of American Popular Music* (New York: Oxford University Press, 2009), 201.

6. For a full discussion of the dialogue between "art" and "authenticity" in pop music and the roots of these mythologies in the Romantic tradition, see Robert Pattison, *The Triumph of Vulgarity: Rock Music in the Mirror of Romanticism* (New York: Oxford University Press, 1987).

7. As discussed by Tim Wall, there is a tradition in journalism that simplistically identifies rock as "good" and pop as "bad." Tim Wall, *Studying Popular Music Culture,* 2nd ed. (London: Sage, 2013).

8. See Simon Napier-Bell, *You Don't Have to Say You Love Me* (London: Ebury Press, 1998), 105–108. See also Johnny Rogan, *Starmakers and Svengalis: The History of British Pop Management* (London: Queen Anne Press, 1988), 183–184.

9. According to the 2020 adjusted ranking in Box Office Mojo, it is the seventh highest grossing (the second pop musical on that list, following *Grease*), and the eighty-sixth film on that table, with actual earnings of $112,892,319.

10. For a series of essays on the phenomenon see Jeffrey Andrew Weinstock, *Reading Rocky Horror: The Rocky Horror Picture Show and Popular Culture* (New York: Springer, 2008).

11. *Newsweek* called it "tasteless, plotless and pointless," cited in Caroline Joan S. Picart, *Remaking the Frankenstein Myth on Film: Between Laughter and Horror* (Albany: State University of New York Press, 2003).

12. David Evans and Scott Michaels, *Rocky Horror: From Concept to Cult* (London: Sanctuary, 2002).

13. J. Hoberman and Jonathan Rosenbaum, *Midnight Movies* (New York: Da Capo Press, 2009), 174–213.

14. For an account of the origins and the mythologies of glam rock, see Simon Reynolds, *Shock and Awe: Glam Rock and Its Legacy, from the Seventies to the Twenty-First Century* (London: Faber & Faber, 2016).

15. Such emphasis on theatricality is one of the pillars of queer camp, and logically the film has become a perfect example of the style as it was expressed in the early seventies. The fact that such expression does not identify with a post-Stonewall agenda, and does not engage with the logic of "positive images" that would become one of the characteristics of later, similar projects, makes it even more relevant for non-gay identifying audiences and is one of the reasons why even now it does not seem old-fashioned.

16. Tom Ryan, *Baz Luhrmann: Interviews* (Jackson: University Press of Mississippi, 2014), 61.

17. Ryan, *Baz Luhrmann*, 60.

18. Ryan, *Baz Luhrmann*, 75.

19. The film refers to three "classic," non-pop songs: it uses a snippet of Rodgers and Hammerstein's "The Sound of Music," sections of "Diamonds Are a Girl's Best Friend" (bridging Marilyn Monroe and Madonna), and Nat King Cole's "Nature Boy" as adapted by David Bowie. The rest of the selection ranges from 1970 (Elton John's "Your Song") to Nirvana's 1991 "Smells Like Teen Spirit" and the 1998 Bollywood song "Chamma Chamma."

20. For an overview of the evolution of dance in musicals, see Beth Genné, *Dance Me a Song: Astaire, Balanchine, Kelly, and the American Film Musical* (New York: Oxford University Press, 2018).

21. Hostility to disco from the traditional "rock" institutions was as intense as the devotion of its fans.

22. Barry Keith Grant, *The Hollywood Film Musical* (Chichester, UK: John Wiley & Sons, 2012), 99–115.

23. Although listed as co-director, Robbins did little work for the film after shooting the "Prologue," "America," and "Cool" musical numbers.

24. Simon Frith, "The Best Disco Record: Sharon Redd: 'Never Give You Up,'" in *Beautiful Things in Popular Culture*, ed. Alan McKee (Malden, Mass.: John Wiley & Sons, 2008), 200.

25. Richard Dyer, "In Defense of Disco," *New Formations* 58, no. 58 (1979): 101–108.

26. Frith, "The Best Disco Record," 196.

27. Nelson George, *Hip Hop America* (New York: Viking Penguin, 2005), 14–21.

28. In *Something From Nothing: The Art of Rap* (2012).

29. Jeff Chang, *Can't Stop Won't Stop: A History of the Hip Hop Generation* (New York: Picador, 2005).

30. For a detailed analysis of Baby's learning montage that considers the relationship between movement, music, and mise en scène, see Lesley Vize, "Music and the Body in Dance Film," in *Popular Music and Film*, ed. Ian Inglis (London: Wallflower Press, 2003).

31. Jane Feuer, "Is *Dirty Dancing* a Musical, and Why Should it Matter?," in *The Time of Our Lives: Dirty Dancing and Popular Culture*, ed. Yannis Tzioumakis and Siân Lincoln (Detroit: Wayne State University Press, 2013), 59–72.

32. The films are *Coal Miner's Daughter* (1980), *Ray* (2004), *Walk the Line* (2005), and *Bohemian Rhapsody* (2019).

33. For a more comprehensive list of film and TV music biopics, see Ian Inglis, "Popular Music History on Screen: The Pop/Rock Biopic," *Popular Music History* 2, no. 1 (2007): 78–79.

34. For instance, the first cycle of pop biopics focused on the lives of country singers, and their approaches to music and narrative were simplistic. For a discussion of these, see Bruce Babington, "Star Personae and Authenticity in the Country Music Biopic," in *Film's Musical Moments*, ed. Ian Conrich and Estella Tincknell (Edinburgh: Edinburgh University Press, 2006), 84–98.

35. As Ian Inglis says, the reason why the pop biopics can err on the bland side is that "popular music is still a young popular form—barely fifty years old. And as many of its more celebrated (or notorious) performers are alive and well—well enough to issue writs or threaten to sue—there may have been sound legal reasons for studios seeking to steer clear of potentially sensitive and litigious scenarios." Inglis, "Popular Music History on Screen," 79.

36. See Lee Marshall and Isabel Kongsgaard, "Representing Popular Music Stardom on Screen: The Popular Music Biopic," *Celebrity Studies* 3, no. 3 (2012): 346–361.

37. See Susan Smith, *The Musical* (New York: Wallflower Press, 2005), 106–116.

38. Jesse Schlotterbeck, " 'Trying to Find a Heartbeat': Narrative Music in the Pop Performer Biopic," *Journal of Popular Film and Television* 36, no. 2 (2008): 84–85.

39. Elton John, *Me* (New York: MacMillan, 2019).

40. Tom Doyle, *Captain Fantastic: Elton John's Stellar Trip Through the '70s* (New York: Ballantine Books, 2017).

41. Reed is here depicted as a "villain." This further illustrates Marshall and Kongsgaard's argument about the biopic requiring strict narrative conventions, rather than just following life events. Elton's own assessment in his memoir *Me* is less simplistic. Marshall and Kongsgaard, "Representing Popular Music Stardom on Screen," 346–361.

3. Looking Back: The Pop Musical and the Past

1. Simon Reynolds, *Shock and Awe: Glam Rock and Its Legacy, from the Seventies to the Twenty-First Century* (London: Faber & Faber, 2016), 283.

2. See Michael D. Dwyer, *Back to the Fifties: Nostalgia, Hollywood Film, and Popular Music of the Seventies and Eighties* (New York: Oxford University Press, 2015), for a discussion of the evolution of the nostalgia craze in the 1970s.

3. One of the legacies that post-1940 musical theatre handed down through the following decades was that musicals set in the past needed to use "correct" styles, and gesture towards the music being heard at the time. This was particularly true of Broadway shows: Sondheim's *Follies* tried to recreate the sounds of the pre-war era; *Ragtime* reconstructed the melting pot of music styles in the 1910s. This general notion extended to shows set in the pop music era, which had to do the same.

4. The use of the pop styles in *Little Shop of Horrors* allows the film to signify different things, to intensify its sense of irony and history. The musical and the film are set somewhere after 1960, before John F. Kennedy's assassination in 1963.

5. Dwyer, *Back to the Fifties*, 4–13.

6. Rick Altman actually places *Grease* in the "folk" subgenre. Still, the structural similarities with the operetta are also clear and Altman himself seems aware of it. See Rick Altman, *The American Film Musical* (Bloomington: Indiana University Press, 1988), 108 and 378.

7. The original was very much an ensemble piece, with songs evenly distributed across the whole cast.

8. See Robert Hofler, *Party Animals: A Hollywood Tale of Sex, Drugs, and Rock 'n' Roll Starring the Fabulous Allan Carr* (New York: Da Capo Press, 2010); Stephen Tropiano, *Rebels and Chicks: A History of the Hollywood Teen Movie* (New York: Backstage Books, 2006).

9. Eve Arden had created a sarcastic persona in the 1940s, in brief appearances in films such as *Ziegfeld Girl* (1941), and was Oscar nominated for a similar role in *Mildred Pierce* (1945). Joan Blondell, a star of several Busby Berkley musicals, had one of her earliest roles as a waitress.

10. The soundtrack to *Grease* was the second best-selling album in the history of the film musical. *Saturday Night Fever* took the top position. See Stephen Tropiano, *Grease: Music on Film Series* (Lanham, Md.: Limelight Editions, 2011).

11. In the original stage incarnation, Rizzo's pregnancy was left unresolved.

12. For an extensive discussion of Motown's politics, see Suzanne E. Smith, *Dancing in the Street: Motown and the Cultural Politics of Detroit* (Cambridge, Mass.: Harvard University Press, 2009).

13. Timothy N. Laurie, "Come Get These Memories: Gender, History, and Racial Uplift in Bill Condon's *Dreamgirls*," *Social Identities* 18, no. 5 (2012): 538. See also Susan Smith, *The Musical: Race, Gender and Performance* (London: Wallflower Press, 2005), for a discussion on the workings of stereotyping in classical musicals.

14. See Jane Feuer, "The Self-Reflective Musical and the Myth of Entertainment," in *Hollywood Musicals, the Film Reader*, ed. Steven Cohan (Routledge: London, 2002), 31–40.

15. In the documentary *Building the Dream*, director Bill Condon explains how he was so excited by his memories of one particular costume change during the song "I Am Changing," that he decided to pay tribute to it in the way he shot the song.

16. Nelson George, *Hip Hop America* (New York: Viking Penguin, 1998), 44.

17. Michael Bennett himself insisted he wanted to tell a story about "Americans." See Ken Mandelbaum, *A Chorus Line and the Musicals of Michael Bennett* (New York: St. Martin's Press, 1989), 217.

18. See Kevin Kelly, *One Singular Sensation: The Michael Bennett Story* (New York: St. Martin's Press, 1990), 226, for ways in which the show attempted to distance itself from the Supremes story.

19. Marvin Gaye had to overcome Gordy's reluctance to release his socially aware LP *What's Going On?*.

20. Laurie, "Come Get These Memories," 549.

21. See, for instance, Jaap Kooijman, "Fierce, Fabulous, and In/Famous: Beyoncé as Black Diva," *Popular Music and Society* 42, no. 1, (2019): 7, for a summary of these objections.

22. Not coincidentally, some of the issues in this relationship mirror the ones between Ike and Tina Turner as analyzed by Susan Smith in her discussion of the film *What's Love Got to Do with It*. See Smith, *The Musical*, 106–116.

23. Laurie, "Come Get These Memories," 540.

24. Jaap Kooijman, "Whitewashing the Dreamgirls: Beyoncé, Diana Ross, and the Commodification of Blackness," in *Revisiting Star Studies: Cultures, Themes and Methods*, ed. Sabrina Qiong Yu and Guy Austin (Edinburgh: Edinburgh University Press, 2017),105–108.

25. See Frank W. Hoffmann, "Popular Music and Its Relationship to Black Social Consciousness," *Popular Music and Society* 8, no. 3–4 (1982): 55–61, for further examples of cultural appropriation.

26. Kelly, *One Singular Sensation*, 226.

27. In the London 2015 production of the show, the song is kept as a duet in which both Deena and Effie ask the other to listen to their side of the story.

28. Written originally as a solo for Beyoncé, the song has now been included in new stage productions of *Dreamgirls* as a duet between Deena and Effie.

29. Chad Bennett, "Flaming the Fans: Shame and the Aesthetics of Queer Fandom in Todd Haynes's *Velvet Goldmine*," *Cinema Journal* 49, no. 2 (2010): 17–39.

30. Todd Haynes and James Lyons, *Velvet Goldmine* (London: Faber & Faber, 1998), xvii.

31. Stephen N. doCarmo, "Beyond Good and Evil: Mass Culture Theorized in Todd Haynes' Velvet Goldmine," *Journal of American & Comparative Cultures* 25, no. 3-4 (2002): 395.

32. See Reynolds, *Shock and Awe*, 322.

33. Rumors that the therapy was intended to curb homosexual tendencies were dispelled by Reed's sister after his death.

34. Haynes and Lyons, *Velvet Goldmine*, xiii.

35. Haynes and Lyons, *Velvet Goldmine*, xvi.

36. Sean Griffin, *Free and Easy? A Defining History of the American Film Musical Genre* (Oxford: John Wiley & Sons, 2017), 217 and 259.

37. From the published script: Haynes and Lyons, *Velvet Goldmine*, 15. The statement can be confronted with a similar one by Lou Reed around 1972: "a style thing . . . like platform shoes . . . the notion that everybody's bisexual is a very popular line right now, but I think its validity is limited. I could say something like if in any way my album helps people decide who or what they are they, I will feel I have accomplished something in my life. But I don't feel that way at all. I don't think an album's gonna do anything. You can't listen to a record and say, 'Oh that really turned me onto gay life, I'm gonna be gay.' A lot of people will have one or two experiences and that'll be it."

38. Reynolds, *Shock and Awe*, 276.

39. Bennett, "Flaming the Fans," 28.

40. Discussing songs from a very different musical subgenre—taken from his experience of American musical theatre—D. A. Miller reaches, in *Place for Us*, a similar diagnostic on how popular music becomes the language in which certain experiences of marginalization can be expressed and shared. See D. A. Miller, *Place for Us: Essay on the Broadway Musical* (Cambridge, Mass.: Harvard University Press, 1998).

BIBLIOGRAPHY

Altman, Rick. *The American Film Musical*. Bloomington: Indiana University Press, 1987.

Altschuler, Glenn C. *All Shook Up: How Rock 'n' Roll Changed America*. New York: Oxford University Press, 2003.

Babington, Bruce. "Star Personae and Authenticity in the Country Music Biopic." In *Film's Musical Moments*, ed. Ian Conrich and Estella Tinknell, 84–98. Edinburgh: Edinburgh University Press, 2006.

Babington, Bruce, and Peter William Evans. *Blue Skies and Silver Linings: Aspects of the Hollywood Musical*. Manchester: Manchester University Press, 1988.

Baker, David. "Rock Rebels and Delinquents: The Emergence of the Rock Rebel in 1950s 'Youth Problem' Films." *Continuum. Journal of Media and Cultural Studies* 19, no. 1 (2005): 39–54.

Bennett, Chad. "Flaming the Fans: Shame and the Aesthetics of Queer Fandom in Todd Haynes's *Velvet Goldmine*." *Cinema Journal* 49, no. 2 (2010): 17–39.

Bennett, Tony, Simon Frith, Lawrence Grossberg, John Shepherd, and Graeme Turner, eds. *Rock and Popular Music: Politics, Policies, Institutions*. London: Routledge, 2005.

Block, Geoffrey. *Enchanted Evenings: The Broadway Musical from "Show Boat" to Sondheim and Lloyd Webber*. New York: Oxford University Press, 2009.

Bourdieu, Pierre. *Distinction: A Social Critique of the Judgement of Taste*, trans. Richard Nice. Cambridge, Mass.: Harvard University Press, 1984.

Brackett, David. "The Politics and Practice of 'Crossover' in American Popular Music, 1963 to 1965." *Musical Quarterly* 78, no. 4 (1994): 774–797.

Bunch, Ryan. "'Love Is an Open Door': Revising and Repeating Disney's Musical Tropes in Frozen." In *Contemporary Musical Film*, ed. Kevin J. Donnelly and Beth Carroll, 89–103. Edinburgh: Edinburgh University Press, 2017.

Calavita, Marco. "'MTV Aesthetics' at the Movies: Interrogating a Film Criticism Fallacy." *Journal of Film and Video* 59, no. 3 (2007): 15–31.

Casper, Joseph Andrew. *Vincente Minnelli and the Film Musical*. New York: AS Barnes, 1977.

Chambers, Iain. *Urban Rhythms: Pop Music and Popular Culture*. London: Macmillan, 1985.

Chang, Jeff. *Can't Stop Won't Stop: A History of the Hip-Hop Generation*. New York: St. Martin's Press, 2005.

Clarke, Donald. *The Rise and Fall of Popular Music*. London: Viking, 1995.

Coase, Ronald H. "Payola in Radio and Television Broadcasting." *Journal of Law & Economics* 22, no. 2 (1979): 269–328.

Cohan, Steven, ed. *Hollywood Musicals, The Film Reader*. London: Routledge, 2002.

——. *Incongruous Entertainment: Camp, Cultural Value, and the MGM Musical*. Durham, N.C.: Duke University Press, 2005.

Cooper, B. Lee. "Before Elvis: The Prehistory of Rock 'n' Roll." *Rock Music Studies* 1, no. 1 (2015): 97–99.

Crenshaw, Marshall. *Hollywood Rock*. New York: Harper Perennial, 1994.

DoCarmo, Stephen N. "Beyond Good and Evil: Mass Culture Theorized in Todd Haynes' Velvet Goldmine." *Journal of American & Comparative Cultures* 25, no. 3–4 (2002): 395–398.

Donnelly, Kevin J. *Magical Musical Tour: Rock and Pop in Film Soundtracks*. London: Bloomsbury Publishing USA, 2015.

Donnelly, Kevin J., and Beth Carroll, eds. *Contemporary Musical Film*. Edinburgh: Edinburgh University Press, 2017.

Doyle, Tom. *Captain Fantastic: Elton John's Stellar Trip Through the '70s*. New York: Ballantine Books, 2017.

Dwyer, Michael D. *Back to the Fifties: Nostalgia, Hollywood Film, and Popular Music of the Seventies and Eighties*. New York: Oxford University Press, 2015.

Dyer, Richard. *Only Entertainment*, 1st ed. London: Routledge, 1992.

——. "In Defense of Disco." *New Formations* 58, no. 58 (1979): 101–108.

——. *In the Space of a Song: The Uses of Song in Film*. London: Routledge, 2012.

Everett, William A., and Paul R. Laird, eds. *The Cambridge Companion to the Musical*. Cambridge: Cambridge University Press, 2002.

Feuer, Jane. *The Hollywood Musical*. London: Macmillan, 1993.

——. "Is Dirty Dancing a Musical, and Why Should It Matter?" In *The Time of Our Lives: Dirty Dancing and Popular Culture*, ed. Yannis Tzioumakis and Siân Lincoln, 59–72. Detroit: Wayne State University Press, 2013.

Fraser, Benson P., and William J. Brown. "Media, Celebrities, and Social Influence: Identification with Elvis Presley." *Mass Communication and Society* 5, no. 2 (2002): 183–206.

Friedlander, Paul. *Rock and Roll: A Social History*. Boulder, Colo.: Westview Press, 1996.

Frith, Simon. *Music for Pleasure: Essays in the Sociology of Pop*. New York: Routledge, 1988.

Garcia, Desirée J. *The Migration of Musical Film: From Ethnic Margins to American Mainstream*. New Brunswick, N.J.: Rutgers University Press, 2014.

Genné, Beth. *Dance Me a Song: Astaire, Balanchine, Kelly, and the American Film Musical*. New York: Oxford University Press, 2018.

George, Nelson. *Hip Hop America*. New York: Viking Penguin, 2005.

——. *Post-Soul Nation: The Explosive, Contradictory, Triumphant, and Tragic 1980s as Experienced by African Americans (Previously Known as Blacks and Before That Negroes)*. New York: Viking Penguin, 2005.

Grant, Barry K. "The Classic Hollywood Musical and the 'Problem' of Rock 'n' Roll." *Journal of Popular Film and Television* 13, no. 4 (1986): 195–205.

——. *The Hollywood Film Musical*. Chichester, UK: John Wiley & Sons, 2012.

Grant, Mark N. *The Rise and Fall of the Broadway Musical*. Hanover, N.H.: University Press of New England, 2004.

Green, Stanley. *Encyclopaedia of the Musical Film*. New York: Oxford University Press, 1981.

Gridley, Mark C. "Clarifying Labels: Jazz, Rock, Funk, and Jazz-Rock." *Popular Music and Society* 9, no. 2 (1983): 27–34.

Griffin, Sean. *Free and Easy? A Defining History of the American Film Musical Genre*. Oxford: John Wiley & Sons, 2017.

Grossberg, Lawrence. "Putting the Pop Back into Postmodernism." *Social Text*, no. 21 (1989): 167–190.

Haynes, Todd, and James Lyons. *Velvet Goldmine*. London: Faber & Faber, 1998.

Hebdige, Dick. "Subculture: The Meaning of Style." *Critical Quarterly* 37, no. 2 (1995): 120–124.

Heldt, Guido. *Music and Levels of Narration in Filmnull*. Exeter, UK: Intellect Books, 2013.

Hirschhorn, Clive. *The Hollywood Musical*. New York: Crown, 1981.

Hoberman, J., and Jonathan Rosenbaum. *Midnight Movies*. New York: Da Capo Press, 2009.

Hoffmann, Frank W. "Popular Music and Its Relationship to Black Social Consciousness." *Popular Music and Society* 8, no. 3–4 (1982): 55–61.

Hofler, Robert. *Party Animals: A Hollywood Tale of Sex, Drugs, and Rock 'n' Roll Starring the Fabulous Allan Carr*. New York: Da Capo Press, 2010.

Inglis, Iain, ed. *Popular Music and Film*. London: Wallflower Press, 2003.

——. "Popular Music History on Screen: The Pop/Rock Biopic." *Popular Music History* 2, no. 1 (2007): 77–93.

James, David E. *Rock 'n' Film: Cinema's Dance with Popular Music*. New York: Oxford University Press, 2015.

——. "Rock 'n' Film: Generic Permutations in Three Feature Films from 1964." *Grey Room*, no. 49 (2012): 6–31.

John, Elton. *Me*. New York: Macmillan, 2019.

Kehr, Dave. "Can't Stop the Musicals." *American Film* 9, no. 7 (1984). 33–37.

Kelly, Kevin. *One Singular Sensation: The Michael Bennett Story*. New York: St. Martin's Press, 1990.

Kessler, Kelly. *Destabilizing the Hollywood Musical: Music, Masculinity and Mayhem*. Basingstoke, UK: Palgrave Macmillan, 2010.

Knapp, Raymond. *The American Musical and the Formation of National Identity*. Princeton, N.J.: Princeton University Press, 2005.

Knight, Arthur. *Disintegrating the Musical: Black Performance and American Musical Film*. Durham, N.C.: Duke University Press, 2002.

Kobal, John. *Gotta Sing Gotta Dance: A History of Movie Musicals*. London: Hamlyn, 1983.

Kooijman, Jaap. "Fierce, Fabulous, and In/Famous: Beyoncé as Black Diva." *Popular Music and Society* 42, no. 1 (2019): 6–21.

——. "Whitewashing the Dreamgirls: Beyoncé, Diana Ross, and the Commodification of Blackness." *Revisiting Star Studies: Cultures, Themes and Methods*, ed. Sabrina Qiong Yu and Guy Austin, 105–124. Edinburgh: Edinburgh University Press, 2017.

Laurie, Timothy N. "Come Get These Memories: Gender, History, and Racial Uplift in Bill Condon's *Dreamgirls*." *Social Identities* 18, no. 5 (2012): 537–553.

Lobalzo Wright, Julie. *Crossover Stardom: Popular Male Music Stars in American Cinema*. New York: Bloomsbury Publishing USA, 2017.

Loy, Stephen, Julie Rickwood, and Samantha Bennett. "Popular Music, Stars and Stardom: Definitions, Discourses, Interpretations." In *Popular Music, Stars and Stardom*, ed. Stephen Loy, Julie Rickwood, and Samantha Bennett, 1–20. Acton, Australia: ANU Press, 2018.

Lull, James. *Popular Music and Communication*. Newbury Park, Calif.: Sage, 1992.

MacKinnon, Kenneth. "'I Keep Wishing I Were Somewhere Else': Space and Fantasies of Freedom in the Hollywood Musical." In *Musicals: Hollywood and Beyond*, ed. Bill Marshall and Robynn Stilwell, 40–46. Exeter, UK: Intellect Books, 2000.

Mandelbaum, Ken. *A Chorus Line and the Musicals of Michael Bennett*. New York: St. Martin's Press, 1989.

Marcus, Greil. *Mystery Train: Images of America in Rock 'n' Roll Music*. New York: Penguin, 2015.

Marshall, Bill, and Robynn J. Stilwell. *Musicals: Hollywood and Beyond*. Exeter, UK: Intellect Books, 2000.

Marshall, Lee, and Isabel Kongsgaard. "Representing Popular Music Stardom on Screen: The Popular Music Biopic." *Celebrity Studies* 3, no. 3 (2012): 346–361.

McKee, Alan, ed. *Beautiful Things in Popular Culture*. Malden, Mass.: John Wiley & Sons, 2008.

McMillin, Scott. *The Musical as Drama*. Princeton, N.J.: Princeton University Press, 2014.

Merwe, Ann van der. "Music, the Musical, and Postmodernism in Baz Luhrmann's *Moulin Rouge*." *Music and the Moving Image* 3, no. 3 (2010): 31–38.

Michaels, Scott, and David Evans. *Rocky Horror: From Concept to Cult*. London: Sanctuary, 2002.

Miller, D. A. *Place for Us: Essay on the Broadway Musical*. Cambridge, Mass.: Harvard University Press, 1998.

Monteyne, Kimberley. *Hip Hop on Film: Performance Culture, Urban Space, and Genre Transformation in the 1980s*. Jackson: University Press of Mississippi, 2013.

Mordden, Ethan. *Open a New Window: The Broadway Musical in the 1960s*. New York: St. Martin's Press, 2015.

Morris, Gary. "Beyond the Beach: Social and Formal Aspects of AIP's Beach Party Movies." *Journal of Popular Film and Television* 21, no. 1 (1993): 1–11.

Mueller, John. "Fred Astaire and the Integrated Musical." *Cinema Journal* 24, no. 1 (1984): 28–40.

Napier-Bell, Simon. *You Don't Have to Say You Love Me*. London: Ebury, 1998.

Pattison, Robert. *The Triumph of Vulgarity: Rock Music in the Mirror of Romanticism*. Oxford: Oxford University Press, 1987.

Penner, Nina. "Rethinking the Diegetic/Nondiegetic Distinction in the Film Musical." *Music and the Moving Image* 10, no. 3 (2017): 3–20.

Peterson, Richard A. "Why 1955? Explaining the Advent of Rock Music." *Popular Music* 9, no. 1 (1990): 97–116.

Picart, Caroline Joan S. *Remaking the Frankenstein Myth on Film: Between Laughter and Horror*. Albany: State University of New York Press, 2003.

Radwan, Jon. "A Generic Approach to Rock Film." *Popular Music and Society* 20, no. 2 (1996): 155–171.

Reynolds, Simon. *Shock and Awe: Glam Rock and Its Legacy, from the Seventies to the Twenty-First Century*. London: Faber & Faber, 2016.

Rogan, Johnny. *Starmakers and Svengalis: The History of British Pop Management*. London: Queen Anne Press, 1988.

Rutsky, R. L. "Surfing the Other: Ideology on the Beach." *Film Quarterly* 52, no. 4 (1999): 12–23.

Ryan, Tom. *Baz Luhrmann: Interviews*. Jackson: University Press of Mississippi, 2014.

Schlotterbeck, Jesse. "'Trying to Find a Heartbeat': Narrative Music in the Pop Performer Biopic." *Journal of Popular Film and Television* 36, no. 2 (2009): 82–90.

Smith, Susan. *The Musical: Race, Gender and Performance*. London: Wallflower Press, 2005.

Smith, Suzanne E. *Dancing in the Street: Motown and the Cultural Politics of Detroit*. Cambridge, Mass.: Harvard University Press, 2009.

Stanley, Bob. *Yeah Yeah Yeah: The Story of Modern Pop*. London: Faber & Faber, 2013.

Taylor, Joy T. "'You Can't Spend Your Whole Life on a Surfboard': Elvis Presley, Exotic Whiteness, and Native Performance in *Blue Hawaii* and *Girls! Girls! Girls!*" *Quarterly Review of Film and Video* 32, no. 1 (2015): 21–37.

Tinkcom, Matthew. *Working Like a Homosexual: Camp, Capital, Cinema*. Durham, N.C.: Duke University Press, 2002.

Tropiano, Stephen. *Grease: Music on Film Series*. Lanham, Md.: Limelight Editions, 2011.

——. *Rebels and Chicks: A History of the Hollywood Teen Movie*. New York: Backstage Books, 2006.

Vize, Lesley. "Music and the Body in Dance Film." In *Popular Music and Film*, ed. Iain Inglis, 22–39. London: Wallflower, 2003.

Wald, Elijah. *How the Beatles Destroyed Rock 'n' Roll: An Alternative History of American Popular Music*. New York: Oxford University Press, 2009.

Wall, Tim. *Studying Popular Music Culture*. 2nd ed. London: Sage, 2013.

Warfield, Scott. "From Hair to Rent: Is 'Rock' a Four-Letter Word on Broadway?" In *The Cambridge Companion to the Musical*, 1st ed., ed. William A. Everett and Paul R. Laird, 231–245. Cambridge: Cambridge University Press, 2002.

Weinstock, Jeffrey Andrew. *Reading Rocky Horror: The Rocky Horror Picture Show and Popular Culture*. New York: Springer, 2008.

Wollman, Elizabeth L. *The Theater Will Rock: A History of the Rock Musical, from Hair to Hedwig*. Ann Arbor: University of Michigan Press, 2006.

INDEX

SHORT CUTS

INTRODUCTIONS TO FILM STUDIES